The Two Sides of the
GOLDEN RULE

LIVING ASSERTIVELY IS LIVING BIBLICALLY

The Two Sides of the
GOLDEN RULE

MARTHA FEHR, M.A. *with* WES FEHR, PH.D.

WestBow
PRESS
A DIVISION OF THOMAS NELSON

WestBow Press books may be ordered through booksellers or by contacting:

WestBow Press
A Division of Thomas Nelson
1663 Liberty Drive
Bloomington, IN 47403
www.westbowpress.com
1-(866) 928-1240

Scripture taken from the King James Version of the Holy Bible.

Scripture taken from the New King James Version. Copyright 1979, 1980, 1982 by Thomas Nelson, inc. Used by permission. All rights reserved.

Scripture taken from the HOLY BIBLE, NEW INTERNATIONAL VERSION®. Copyright © 1973, 1978, 1984 Biblica. Used by permission of Zondervan. All rights reserved.

Scripture quotations are taken from the Holy Bible, New Living Translation, copyright 1996, 2004. Used by permission of Tyndale House Publishers, Inc., Wheaton, Illinois 60189. All rights reserved.

Scripture quotations taken from the New American Standard Bible®, Copyright © 1960, 1962, 1963, 1968, 1971, 1972, 1973, 1975, 1977, 1995 by The Lockman Foundation Used by permission. (www.Lockman.org)

Scripture taken from the New Century Version. Copyright © 1987, 1988, 1991 by Thomas Nelson, Inc. Used by permission. All rights reserved.

ISBN: 978-1-4497-1317-1 (sc)
ISBN: 978-1-4497-1318-8 (e)

Library of Congress Control Number: 2011923713

Printed in the United States of America

WestBow Press rev. date: 3/14/2011

Contents

Foreword

Dr. Wes Fehr and Martha Fehr are counselors at Lifeline Counselling, the practice they established in 1989. Dr. Fehr specializes in working with couples who are experiencing marital difficulties. Martha works with individuals who are dealing with anxiety, depression, abuse and self-esteem issues.

This book comes at the request of some of the clients we have worked with over the years we have been in counseling. We have learned much about the need for assertiveness by observing how destructive it is when people are passive, aggressive, or even passive/aggressive.

Most people are familiar with the Golden Rule even when they don't realize it comes from the Bible. Matthew 7:12 says, "Do to others what you would have them do to you." How do we want others to treat us? I believe the word "respect" best describes how we want to be treated, and how we should treat others. Asking for that respect is as important as giving that respect to others and results in behaving assertively.

This explains the diagram on the cover. Apples and oranges are both good for us so the scale is evenly balanced. If we learn to ask for respect as well as give respect to others, we will be living healthy, assertive and balanced lives. This book is an attempt to show you how to do this in very practical ways. We believe living assertively will result in a healthy self-esteem, improved interpersonal relationships and a more intimate relationship with God.

Case studies may be a compilation of several different people that we have seen over the years, either in our personal life, in the office, or they may be totally fictional.

We would like to dedicate this book to all the wonderful people we have had the privilege of meeting in our counseling office.

Part I

INTRODUCTION

Chapter I
VIGNETTES

Louise shifted her body noisily as she turned over once more and slammed her fist into the pillow. Then she raised her head, grabbed the pillow and turned it over; the pillow was wet with tears and sleep would not come. Over and over, she relived what had happened earlier in the day.

Louise was living with her married son and daughter-in-law since separating from her husband. She had always been insecure as a child, and when she met Tom during her first year in college, she was flattered at the attention he gave her. The two of them had dated steadily in the months that followed, and Louise had quickly fallen in love with Tom. Several times during their months of dating, Tom had angrily lashed out at Louise for something she had done. Louise was used to second-guessing her own ideas and actions, so she had quickly apologized to Tom and he had settled down. When Tom proposed after six months of dating, Louise said, "Yes!"

Tom continued his domineering ways in the marriage and Louise retreated further and further into her shell; she let Tom make all the decisions and accepted his verbal abuse. The more that Louise withdrew, the more dominant Tom became.

Somehow Louise carried on and the two of them raised three children, all of whom were now married.

One day when Tom was having a fit of anger, he reached out and shoved Louise so that she fell and bruised her arm on the coffee table which she hit on her way to the floor. When her son Mike, stopped in the next day and saw her bruises, she tried to convince him that she had tripped on the vacuum cleaner cord, causing her to fall and bruise her arm on the coffee table.

Mike had seen his father's angry outbursts often enough that he was not convinced, and insisted that she come and stay with them for awhile. When Tom returned to an empty house, he got so angry that Louise knew it would not be safe for her to return home and with her son's encouragement; she started proceedings for a legal separation. She had been living with Mike and his wife for the last two months now.

Louise had agreed to meet Tom at a restaurant earlier that day where Tom had told her that he had decided to list their home for sale. Since she had been the one to leave, he said she would no longer be entitled to any of the proceeds. Now Louise couldn't stop thinking about how unfair Tom was being. She had worked hard over the years, putting Tom through business training and continuing to work until he was able to start his own business and was established with a reliable client base. Now she stood to lose everything she had worked for so hard. She still loved Tom but now she would not only lose him, she would lose her home and everything that was part of her material world.

Louise was not aware of the legality of what Tom told her, and once again, she assumed he was right to claim all the proceeds of the sale, and felt she would need to settle for getting nothing. But the bare facts were not the only things upsetting Louise; she couldn't forget how demeaning Tom had been when he spoke to her at the restaurant, and to make matters worse, it seemed that he had actually been flirting with the waitress every time she came to wait on them. Try as she might, Louise could not get the conversation out of her mind and sleep was impossible. The last time she saw the alarm clock it read 3:34 a.m.

The next thing she knew, the alarm went off at 6:30 and she needed to get up. She had barely opened her eyes when the sadness came back like a heavy blanket that was suffocating her. Louise didn't know how she would get through the day...

Jack had been raised with an angry, domineering father who never let him express his own ideas or feelings. As a result, a simmering anger grew within Jack and he was quick to take it out on unsuspecting people. Jack was especially mean to people in positions of weakness.

When Jack grew up, he became an accountant and started to work for an important company in his city. Jack soon worked his way up to a managerial position; he was very good at what he did but he had very little patience with the people he supervised. Jack would assign projects to the other accountants; then it would be his responsibility to review their work. Jack demanded perfection and reprimanded anyone whose work was not perfect. Over the years with this company, several of the accountants under Jack's supervision decided to leave the company with rather flimsy excuses. Only Jack seemed oblivious to the fact that the real reason these people were leaving was due to his angry tirades and his impatience with them.

After several years with the company, the employer decided to implement a review plan whereby every employee would be evaluated by everyone else who worked in the same department. This meant that while Jack was free to evaluate the accountants under him; these same accountants would be evaluating him.

The day came for the results of Jack's evaluation to be reviewed. Everyone in Jack's department along with their employer gathered in the board room; all evaluations had been turned in without signatures. Solemnly, the employer began to read the evaluations which revealed that his co-workers saw Jack as an angry, impatient person. They also said that he was intimidating and degrading, often putting them down in front of their fellow accountants. Jack listened to these evaluations with astonishment and sensed his anger rising within. He wanted to strike out and hit someone or something, and when the meeting ended, he stalked out of the room without a word. Inside Jack was stewing and inwardly he was beginning to plan his revenge. They would be sorry they had dared to say those things! Didn't they know that without his expertise, the company would be struggling to compete in the business market!

When Jack walked in the door of his home, the first thing he saw was his son's tricycle in the middle of the living room. He grabbed the trike, opened the front door, and threw it onto the lawn. His two year old son started wailing, and Jack responded by swatting him hard across his face. Jack's wife came running into the room and tried to pick up their son but Jack yelled at her to leave him alone, saying he deserved to be punished. Next, he proceeded to lecture his wife for allowing their son to bring the tricycle inside. Jack told his wife he needed some quiet time and retired to his study to plan how he would get his revenge on his co-workers. Needless to say, the rest of the evening in this household, was not a happy one! …

Samantha was a spoiled brat. At 16, she was an only child and since her mother worked at a well paying job, she got pretty much everything she ever asked for. Samantha knew that her mother was trying to make it up to her for having divorced her father, a loser who didn't bother to keep in touch with either of them. Samantha also got to do pretty much whatever she wanted. She often hung around with a wild bunch of kids and attended parties at which there were drugs and alcohol. As lenient as her mother was, she did draw the line at those kinds of parties, so Samantha lied frequently, pretending to go to her girlfriend's house for a sleepover.

One day Samantha's friend Julie, asked her to go to a concert in another city. Samantha asked her mother if she could go, assuming it would be easy to get her permission. However, this time was different. Samantha's mother asked who would be driving, and when she found out it was Judd, a grade 11 kid who was notorious for smashing up his parent's car, she refused to let Samantha go. Samantha protested loudly and physically attacked her mother.

To protect herself, Samantha's mother pinned her to the floor and sat on her. She explained the dangers of riding with someone who had Judd's reputation, trying to reason with Samantha but to no avail. Samantha argued that if Julie felt safe driving with Judd, surely all would be well. Samantha's mother asked her to think about it and when Samantha promised that she would, her mother got up and let Samantha get up as well.

Samantha had no intention of changing her mind about attending the concert. She had always had her own way, and nothing would stop her this time; she simply had to come up with a plan. Her first plan involved giving her mother the silent treatment. She would not talk to her mother and soon her mother would feel so guilty for upsetting her, that she would give in. This had always worked in the past. Samantha's mother looked sad at being left out of her daughter's usual happy chatter, but she didn't change her mind. Next, Samantha tried to manipulate her mother by offering to help with the household chores. She even scrubbed the kitchen floor on Saturday before going to the mall with her friends. But every time she brought up the concert, her mother shook her head and told her she had not changed her mind.

The date of the concert was drawing near and Samantha was desperate to find a way of getting to the concert with her friends. The day of the concert, she got into a fight with her mother once more. It started out as a verbal fight but soon Samantha lost control and shoved her mother. Her mother told her there was no point in discussing it further and she simply left the room, telling her once again, that she couldn't go to the concert.

Samantha stomped angrily out of the house and walked down the street, nursing her angry feelings. There must be something she could do! Then she saw it; the local police station was two blocks from their house and she knew just what she would do. Her mother would be sorry for trying to keep her from going to the concert! Samantha ran down the sidewalk and entered the police station. There she found an officer willing to listen to her as she told him that her mother was abusive and that she had just been attacked by her mother who threw her to the floor and sat on her. No matter that this had happened a few weeks earlier and that she had not been hurt. The police officer took her very seriously and called Samantha's grandmother to come and pick her up, after which he went to see her mother. Arriving at Samantha's house, the officer questioned her mother briefly, arrested her, and took her to the station downtown. It didn't take long for the officer to see that he had been duped by Samantha, but he had to follow the rules and so her mother ended up spending the night in jail, totally shocked at what was happening to her.

Samantha told her grandmother that she had plans to spend the evening with her girlfriend and since her grandmother had no way of checking with Samantha's mother, she let her go. On the drive to the concert, Samantha felt powerful and proud of herself for outwitting her mother....

Monica was certainly not perfect, yet she was very content at this time in her life. She was grateful for the many things she had learned and for who she had become. It had been a long journey to get to where she was today, and she knew she needed to continue to grow into the person that God intended for her to be, but right now, she was just grateful for how He had changed her life in the last five years.

Monica had grown up in a very dysfunctional home with parents who hardly knew she existed. When she was sixteen, she ran away from home even though she hated to leave behind her sister Julie, who was only 12. Her desire to reach out and find more in life than what she was getting in her own home, won out in the end. If only she had known that more was not always better! Monica had walked from the frying pan into the fire!

Being tricked into prostitution, getting pregnant, and having to give up her baby for adoption were some of the more difficult things that Monica was forced to deal with in the first year of being away from home.

Monica was also fortunate that even in those dire circumstances, she had found some friends who really cared about her. She found this hard to accept at first since her own parents had not seemed to care if she lived or died. As far as she knew, they had not even tried to find her, even though she had ended up within the borders of the state where her parents and sister continued to live. She reminded herself that she hadn't tried to contact them either, so she tried not to feel too much rejection.

Her newfound friends came to her aid when she discovered her pregnancy. Mary had become a good friend whom she had first met at a Youth Centre. It was through Mary that Monica started attending church and shortly after, she accepted Christ as her personal Savior.

The church offered classes for new believers where the basic elements of faith were discussed and explained and no question was considered off limits. Monica loved this opportunity to explore more of the meaning of life. This basic class was followed by a class teaching life skills as seen through looking at the Bible and following the example of Jesus.

Monica learned about the concept of assertiveness as opposed to being passive, aggressive, or passive/aggressive. She learned that escaping from her pimp had been an assertive action. Even leaving home had been assertive to some extent, although it would have been better to have communicated her intentions to her parents and kept in touch with them.

Monica couldn't bring herself to contact her parents for some time, but eventually she did so with the hope that they would have changed in the meantime. Unfortunately, this was not to be but she did have the opportunity to meet with her sister and make plans for getting together again.

When Monica first started attending church, she assumed that all Christians were really good people and would always treat others in a respectful way. Sad to say, Christians sometimes hurt one another and on several occasions Monica put into practice what she had learned in the church class. She asked the person or persons who had offended her, to sit down and discuss the issue with her. With utmost respect, Monica told them how she felt about their words and actions and asked them not to repeat their behavior in the future.

Some people responded well, often asking for forgiveness. Others became irate and tried to find fault with her behavior. Regardless of their response, Monica assured them of her forgiveness. She had also learned that forgiveness is not the same as restoration of the relationship. Some people were toxic and she did not renew her relationship with them; others changed their behavior and her relationship with them deepened.

Today, Monica is a happy young adult, continuing to learn more about God and His desire for her life...

*   *   *

Louise, Jack and Samantha are all using dysfunctional ways of relating to other people. The answer for all three of them is to learn how to relate assertively which is illustrated by Monica.

When people relate in assertive ways, individuals find purpose and enjoyment in life, couples learn to resolve issues in their marriage, people in the work force treat each other with respect, and parents and children communicate effectively to get along well.

Throughout the book, we will make mention of the people we introduced in the vignettes, and at the end of the book you will be able to read "the rest of their story" for each of them.

There are three main benefits of learning to be assertive. First, behaving assertively improves our self-esteem. With a healthy self-esteem, we are able to act assertively more easily so these two concepts are interchangeable. We do not necessarily need to have a healthy self-esteem to act assertively; we can act assertively even when we are afraid to do so, and we will find that our self-esteem will improve. With this healthy self-esteem and assertive behavior, all of our relationships are healthier; even our relationship with God is deeper and more intimate.

Before we discuss these three benefits of assertiveness in detail, let's take a brief look at different ways of behaving and why assertiveness is so important.

Chapter II
THE FOUR PERSONALITY TYPES

There are generally four ways of relating to others. How you and I relate to others depends a lot on our temperament and our upbringing. The dictionary defines temperament as "a characteristic way of thinking, reacting, or behaving." Disposition, according to the thesaurus, is "... approximately equivalent to one's usual mood, attitude, or frame of mind;" and character refers to the "moral and ethical characteristics..." of a person. Personality, according to the thesaurus, is "... the sum of distinctive qualities and traits of a person that give him his own individuality..."

Since personality seems to include all the aspects of temperament, disposition, and character, we will simply refer to the four personality types. In doing so, we are suggesting that people tend to have four different ways of thinking, acting, reacting and interacting with others.

We have inherited some of these personality traits; other traits have been learned due to observing parents, teachers, and other people in positions of authority. It is very important to understand our own personality type, and to understand that we have the ability to change unhealthy patterns of thinking, acting, and reacting into healthy patterns.

It is also important to recognize that no one fits neatly into one category in all areas. Many of us would find that we have a few characteristics in each of the categories, but we will be more dominant in one.

It is not only helpful to know how to be assertive; it is also helpful to recognize dysfunctional ways of relating. We hope that by explaining all four personality types, you will be able to recognize, and eliminate, dysfunctional ways of relating and learn to relate mostly in assertive ways. Let me explain some of the main differences between the four personality types:

THE PASSIVE PERSONALITY:

The dictionary explains that to be passive is to be "... receiving or enduring without resistance, submissive." This person yields readily to someone else's authority, and in doing so, is not respecting himself.

We tend to think that most passive people are women; however, we have counseled many men who are also passive. In any relationship, it is important that the people in the relationship can have genuine respect for one another. This is especially true in a marriage relationship. When a husband is so passive that his wife has lost her respect for him, she replaces respect with anger and disrespect.

Regardless of the fact that most women are in the workforce and bring home wages similar to their husbands, a woman still wants to feel that her husband has strong opinions and is able to make wise decisions, and can care for her. She desperately wants to be able to respect him.

Sometimes women are passive, mistaking passivity for godly submissiveness to their husbands. Husbands want, and need, the respect of their wives, but they also want their wives to have opinions and to be confident in sharing them.

In the introductory vignettes, Louise is definitely pictured as a passive person. Passive behavior in both men and women is a result of their thinking, attitudes, emotions, and self-view.

THE AGGRESSIVE PERSONALITY:

The dictionary says that, "Aggressive behavior is reactionary and impulsive behavior that often results in breaking household rules, or the law". The behavior is something that happens quickly without consideration for the effect it will have on others; the aggressive person is simply reacting according to how he or she is feeling.

Just as we often think that all passive people are women, we tend to believe that all aggressive people are men. We may picture the aggressive person as towering above others, and using a deep, threatening voice. Again, this is a myth! Both men and women can be aggressive. Big strong men often cower before tiny little spitfire women.

Aggressive people do not respect others and will defend themselves with powerful, nasty behaviors. In the introductory vignettes, Jack has a mostly aggressive personality.

In our office we find that if one spouse in a marriage is aggressive, the other spouse will most often be passive. It seems that the aggressive spouse will look for someone who can be easily dominated.

Again in the introductory vignettes, Louise was married to Tom who was aggressive and domineering. He was likely attracted to her because she was passive, and she easily accepted his domineering characteristics because she had already learned to be passive by growing up with a very domineering father.

THE PASSIVE/AGGRESSIVE PERSONALITY:

Passive/Aggressive behavior according to the dictionary is "... displaying behavior characterized by the expression of negative feelings, resentment, and aggression in an unassertive passive way (as through procrastination and stubbornness)."

This personality type has perhaps the least desirable traits. The passive/aggressive person does not respect others but they are not openly disrespectful; they may appear to be your friend while they are with you, but away from you, they may gossip about you or try to hurt you in some way. The aggressive part of their personality wants to hurt you, but they want to do it in a passive way so that they cannot be held accountable.

Both genders have been found to be guilty of passive/aggressive behavior but in our vignettes, Samantha was the one who had most of the passive/aggressive characteristics.

In our office we use the Taylor-Johnson Temperament Analysis Test for all clients that we see. The test has very specific ways of revealing if a client is mostly passive, aggressive or assertive. When we see a test result showing that the client is mostly passive, yet they have a lot of frustration or anger, we realize that we are probably dealing with someone who is passive/aggressive. This person will often have a test result that shows they also have very high expectations of themselves and others; this usually leads to being highly critical and judgmental of others.

THE ASSERTIVE PERSONALITY:

We believe that assertiveness has been a very misunderstood concept. When some definitions include being able to "stand up" for ourselves, many people immediately visualize an aggressive stance. That is not the true meaning of assertiveness. So what does it really mean?

The dictionary defines assertiveness as "the ability to state your own needs or defend your own personal worth or convictions firmly, without devaluing the needs and feelings of others."

From this definition, we can see that the most important point to remember about behaving assertively is that it requires mutual respect. We should be able to "stand up" for ourselves in a respectful way, while at the same time, seek to understand the other person and their point of view. The assertive person seeks to respect all others in every situation.

The fact that being assertive requires mutual respect is a good indication that the Bible supports assertive behavior. We will look at other ways in which the Bible supports assertiveness.

SELF-TEST RE: WHICH PERSONALITY DO YOU MOST IDENTIFY WITH?

Cover up the answer key and circle the traits that most describe you.

1. I try to gain approval by being compliant.

2. I often give someone the silent treatment.

3. I take charge at times, even if someone else has been asked to take leadership.

4. I can confront issues in a calm manner.

5. I tell people off if they have upset me in some way.

6. I enjoy seeing others fail if they have upset me.

7. I can say "No" without feeling guilty.

8. I try to avoid people who have hurt me in the past.

9. I use "I" sentences which can be firm, but loving.

10. I feel like I need to win every argument.

11. I hold grudges and bring up old issues.

12. I sometimes destroy someone's property to get even.

13. My self-esteem depends on other people's approval.

14. I can take responsibility for my mistakes.

15. I sometimes explode in anger.

16. I often act helpless and let others tell me what to do.

> *#s 4, 7, 9, and 14 are assertive traits
> #s 1, 8, 13 and 16 are passive traits
> #s 2, 6, 11 and 12 are passive/aggressive traits
> #s 3, 5, 10 and 15 are aggressive traits

Where did you check the most traits?

Chapter III
THE IMPORTANCE OF ASSERTIVENESS

Assertiveness is so important because it affects every area of our lives, how we feel about ourselves, how we interact with others, and how we relate to God.

The purpose of this book is to look at the many ways in which assertiveness allows us to enjoy life more fully, according to God's Word.

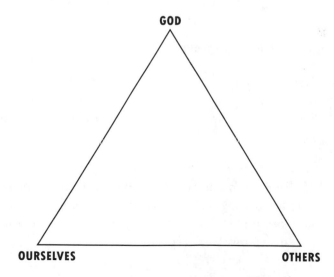

We want to use the illustration of a triangle to help you think about these three areas. Let's allow the bottom left corner of the triangle to represent your relationship with yourself. All of your thoughts, attitudes and emotions combine to form your self-view. When you have a healthy self-view or self-esteem, you will find it easy to reach out to others to have healthy relationships with them, always working to improve your communication skills and being aware of treating others with respect. We'll let the bottom right corner of the triangle represent relationships with others. The top corner represents God; we should always be moving towards God in our relationship with Him, learning to love Him more, hear Him more, and obey Him more. When we are assertive, we feel confident to grow in our relationship with God and confident to share our faith with others. As we draw closer to God and encourage the other person to draw close to God, we will automatically draw closer to each other. This concept is especially important in a marriage relationship, but it also applies to other people. We find that we are closest to friends that also share our faith in God, and with whom we can freely discuss spiritual issues and pray together.

THE BIBLE SUPPORTS ASSERTIVENESS:

If you are a Christian, you may argue that the Bible teaches us to be passive. We believe that if we examine Scripture carefully we will see that assertiveness is the most mature, biblical way of living our lives.

In Ephesians 4:15 we are encouraged to "speak the truth in love." I believe this means we are to speak the truth which may be hard to hear at times, but to do it in a respectful way which will make it easier to bear. In other words, "speaking the truth in love" is an assertive way of speaking.

In the NIV version of Matthew 7:12 we read "…do to others what you would have them do to you…"and in the NASB it reads, "In everything, therefore, treat people the same way you want them to treat you, for this is the law and the Prophets." I believe we want people to treat us with respect and therefore, we need to treat them with respect as well. Again, this would be assertive behavior.

Someone has said that the corollary of the Golden Rule would read, "Don't allow anyone to do to you, what you wouldn't do to them; this has sometimes been called the Silver Rule. This is going one step further than desiring respectful treatment; it is asking for it. The Silver Rule helps us to respect ourselves by refusing to accept disrespectful treatment. If we would strive to live according to the Golden Rule and its Silver companion, we would be living assertively. In simple terms, we would treat all others with respect and we would ask others to treat us with respect.

In this book we want to clearly define assertiveness and compare it with other ways of behaving. If we are not living assertively, perhaps we are being passive, aggressive, or even passive/aggressive. In working with clients, it is very common to find people who have a few characteristics in each category; our goal is always to help clients understand the importance of striving to be assertive in most situations. We do recognize that there are times when it is appropriate to be passive, and there are even times when it is appropriate to be aggressive. Being passive/aggressive is never appropriate.

Learning to be assertive will not mean that you will never have a single problem in your life, but it will definitely help you to handle the difficulties with more confidence and avoid some problems altogether. John 10:10 tells us that Jesus came to give us life and He wants us to "…have it abundantly." This does not mean that we will necessarily enjoy riches, fame, or even good health, but it does mean that with God's help, we will face the challenges of life in a mature, biblical way.

* * *

The presenting problems for most of the clients who come for counseling, is based in problems they encounter in their relationships, be it with family, friends, or co-workers. For this reason, you will notice that the section on assertiveness and relationships is the longest section. However, all three topics impacted by assertiveness, self-esteem, relationships and how we relate to God are so inter-related that I will touch on all three areas in each section, but with a stronger emphasis on one area.

Part II

ASSERTIVENESS BUILDS OUR SELF-ESTEEM

Chapter I
SELF-ESTEEM AND THE BIBLE

Sharon grew up in a strict family with three other sisters. Their parents were immigrants from Germany and they had high expectations for all four girls. Sharon's father was disappointed that he did not have a son whom he could take to ball games or to whom he could pass on his trade of wood-working. Her father spent more time with her sisters because they seemed very confident and they had decided early in life what their career goals would be.

Sharon, on the other hand, seemed shy around her father and preferred to help her mother in the kitchen. She had learned from experience that if she made a mistake while trying to help her father, he would yell, "Can't you do anything right?!"

Helping her mother was better but it was no joy either. Sharon was usually assigned the job of washing dishes but she longed to experiment with recipes. Sharon loved cooking but whenever she started gathering the ingredients for a new recipe, her mother hovered over her, telling her exactly what to do. Even when Sharon was doing something as simple as slicing carrots, her mother would say, "Let me do it, you don't know how."

Today, Sharon is an intelligent, very capable substitute teacher in our city. Why is she a substitute teacher you ask? It is because she continues to second-guess almost everything she does, not trusting her ability to handle a full-time teaching position. Every time Sharon considers taking on a new responsibility, she hears, "Can't you do anything right?' and "Let me do it; you don't know how." These words continue to play like a recording in her head, and most of the time, Sharon takes the easy way out and convinces herself that she prefers to be a part-time, substitute teacher. Sharon struggles with a low self-esteem.

* * *

WHAT IS SELF-ESTEEM?

Barbara Colorosa, best-selling author, mother, teacher and seminar leader agrees with the basic tenet of assertiveness which is respect for everyone. She writes, "Believing kids are worth it, not treating them in a way I would not want to be treated, and behaving in a way that leaves our dignity intact are not themselves specific tools; rather, they provide an attitude and an environment that helps me help my children develop a sense of self-discipline." P.XIV Basically, she is affirming her belief in both the Golden Rule and the Silver Rule.

In her book, kids are worth it!, GIVING YOUR CHILD THE GIFT OF INNER DISCIPLINE, she describes the three aspects of self-esteem: A stands for acceptance; B for belonging; and C for capability. Colorosa speaks to parents and gives them many helpful ways of providing their children with a sense of being accepted, of belonging, and affirming their capability to handle life. As adults we still need to feel accepted, that we belong and that we are capable of handling life.

In his book, Make Anger Your Ally, Neil Warren states his belief that,

"Your self-esteem depends on your getting loved – unconditionally. I can be more precise. The degree to which you are loved unconditionally will determine your level of self-esteem. Unconditional love is absolutely critical." P. 177

He goes on to say that

"Unconditional love has two fundamental qualities: (1) It is given without regard for the objective value of the person or thing which is loved; (2) It is given without any strings or conditions attached."p.177

Where do we get this unconditional love? According to Colorosa, parents should be giving this unconditional love and acceptance to their children. As parents, we find it pretty easy to love our newborns unconditionally, even when they cannot love us in return, and even when they keep us up all night because their tummy hurts. However, many children are still very young when they begin to feel that their parents' love is conditional on their behavior; they receive performance-based acceptance. When parents criticize us or expect too much from us, we don't feel accepted and we begin to doubt our own competence.

Parents can continue to have a strong influence on the child's sense of acceptance with regard to their school performance. Parents need to recognize genuine effort on the part of their children and affirm this rather than expecting high performance from every child. Children should never be compared to their siblings or other children. Every child should be encouraged to do their very best but they should not feel unacceptable if they are unable to perform as well as someone else. Children should be encouraged to recognize their unique abilities which will be different from those of other children.

Teachers have a powerful influence on children and school is once again, a place where performance is rewarded. The kindergarten teacher has brightly colored stickers or stars which she puts on your work when you have colored within the lines. She may also give you a rewarding smile, and you feel acceptance based on how well you performed. This continues through all of our schooling, right through grad school. Of course, the colored stars are replaced with grades and comments on the papers we hand in.

When the messages from our teachers are negative, it can affect our present and our future if we allow it to. When I (Wes) was in grade nine, my teacher came up to my desk one day and caught me day-dreaming. He grabbed me by the ear, yanked me out of my desk, and marched me up to the front of the class. In front of all my classmates, he grabbed both of my ears and bounced me up and down saying, "See this dummy! He can't ever do anything right!" The class laughed and I died a slow death. I was so humiliated that when I walked out of class that afternoon, I vowed to myself that I would never return, not even to clean out my locker. I kept that promise for a number of years.

When I was encouraged to go back to school some time later, my first thoughts were, "No way, I'm a dummy, I can't go back to school." If I had never challenged that thought, I would have continued to let my teacher have power over my way of thinking.

I (Martha) had a negative experience with my elementary school teacher which had a strong effect on me. I grew up in the country and walked three miles (barefoot and uphill both ways!!) to our one-room, red brick school for grades one to eight. The teacher lived in the nearest city with her husband and daughter on the weekends and in the little teacherage during the week. Her daughter Edith lived with her and was in my grade. One summer day, when we were both in grade three, everyone was enjoying the nice weather by playing in the school yard during the noon hour. On the yard was a well with a pump for drawing water. On this day my older brother Jim was moving the pump handle up and down continuously and somehow Edith got her nose bumped in the process. She began to howl and sprinted towards the teacherage. Being a quiet, shy girl, I stayed far back, waiting to see what would happen; had she been seriously hurt? Would Jim get a strapping? With a serious look on my face, I continued to watch the scene at the teacherage, far back from the rest of my classmates. Imagine my surprise when Mrs. Hunter seemed to look right past all the students gathered near the teacherage, straight at me, and with a scowl on her face, she demanded to know why I was laughing about this incident! Then she ordered me to return to the classroom and wait for my strapping! I was so hurt; Edith was my best friend in school next to my sister and I had been truly worried about her injury. Now I was being accused of something I would never do: laugh at my friend's misfortune. What I didn't know as I sat down in my desk was that things would only get worse. When Mrs. Hunter entered the classroom she knelt beside my little desk and gently asked me why I had been laughing. I told her that I had not been laughing but she refused to back down. Looking back on the situation now, I believe she would have lost face before the students in the older grades if she had relented since she had promised to strap me unless I confessed what I had done. After several rounds of accusation and denial, I gave in and admitted that I had laughed at her daughter's pain. Then I apologized for doing so and that was the end of it for Mrs. Hunter, but not for me. I was a Christian even then and it bothered me immensely that I had told a lie; it bothered me even more that a trusted adult, someone I had looked up to, had literally forced me to tell this lie. The memory of that day is vivid even to this day because of the sense of powerlessness it evoked in me.

When we leave the classroom and head out to the real world of jobs and careers and marriage, we find that we will be judged according to our performance once again. Promotions come as a result of excellent work which is as it should be; however, we often tie our value as a person to how well we do in our career, job or relationships. Once again, we are longing for unconditional love and we are afraid we will never find it.

As Christians, we have an advantage over people who do not know God in a personal way; we have God's love letter to us in the Bible which tells us that we are indeed acceptable to God. He loves us just as we are; we do not have to perform for God to earn His love. When we accept His love and forgiveness and invite Jesus to be our Savior, we are not only acceptable to God, now we also belong to the family of God and He has confidence that we will be able to handle all that life throws at us, as we depend on Him.

The problem remains however, that many of us read what the Bible says and we consciously or unconsciously say to ourselves, "That may well apply to my friend at church, but it doesn't apply to me. I've done too many terrible things and if the people at church knew what I've done, they would ask me to leave." Or perhaps our inner dialogue may be, as it was for one of my clients, "I may have been acceptable to God when I was born, but since the neighborhood boy sexually abused me when I was only six years old, I'm no longer acceptable to God."

In Matthew 22:35-40 we have the words of Jesus where He says that we are to "love the Lord your God with all your heart,…" and "love your neighbor as yourself." We cannot properly love God or our fellow man if we don't love ourselves. Why do so many of us find it hard to love ourselves and how can we change that? What does it really mean to love ourselves?

FACTS OR FEELINGS

We are all in a spiritual battle, and Satan wants us to feel badly about ourselves, whispering negative thoughts to us. Because of this, God encourages us in Romans 12:2, "...do not be conformed to this world: but be transformed by the renewing of your mind,..." The world judges us harshly, according to how we perform, but God wants us to realize how special we are, created in His image (Genesis 1:27). When we are encouraged to be transformed by the renewing of our minds, it reveals the importance of our thought life.

It is important to realize that our feelings cannot always be trusted; feelings need to be measured against logic and facts. If we do not **feel** that we are acceptable, that we belong, or that we are capable, we need to examine the **facts** of our acceptance, belonging and capability as explained in the Bible.

Sharon, the teacher, needs to realize that God sees her as a competent teacher who is capable of handling situations in the classroom and in all of life. Wes believed that God had created him with intelligence and he went on to complete a doctorate in biblical counseling. Martha realized she is not powerless and God has given her the opportunity to influence others for Jesus. She is also able to defend herself against people that would try to use her for their own purposes.

Romans 12:3 tells us not to think of ourselves more highly than we ought to think, but to "think soberly". We believe that means that we need to recognize that we all have strengths and weaknesses, and that's okay.

We tend to judge ourselves according to the standards of our society which often base our value on how well we perform, how beautiful we are, how rich we are, or how famous we are. We need to remember what the Bible says in I Samuel 16:7, "... man looks on the outward appearance, but the Lord looks at the heart."

We can say with the Psalmist, "For you formed my inward parts; You covered me in my mother's womb. I will praise You, for I am fearfully and wonderfully made, marvelous are Your works." Psalm 139:13-14. God created us in His image according to Genesis 1:27, and we have no reason whatsoever, to feel badly about ourselves. At the same time, we need to allow Him to continue to mold us and shape us into the image of Jesus Christ as it says in Romans 8:29, "For whom He foreknew, He also predestined to be conformed to the image of His Son...". To become more like Christ we need to believe that we are valuable, worthy people.

When we are tempted to compare ourselves with others, we need to be reminded of what it says in Galatians 6:4 NIV, "Each one should test his own actions. Then he can take pride in himself, without comparing himself to somebody else." When we allow God's Word, and His love for us, to be the standard for our self-esteem, we are basing it on something that is constant and unconditional.

Often, we are our own worst enemy, feeling that unless we are perfect, we have no right to feel good about ourselves. We believe everyone struggles with their self-esteem to some degree, at some time in their lives, due to the pressure put on all of us, by society, family, friends, and ourselves, but we need to accept God's evaluation of us which is "very good" Genesis 1:31.

Chapter II
HOW OUR THOUGHT LIFE AFFECTS OUR SELF-ESTEEM

OUR THOUGHT LIFE

Janet and her two sisters decided to sneak up on their two older brothers who were having a "Boys only," club meeting in their tree house. The girls had been told many times that the tree house belonged to the boys and there would be serious consequences if the girls tried to use it as their playhouse. They were warned to not even get near the tree house when they were using it.

On this particular day, the girls believed that some of the cute guys from the grade six class at their school were at the meeting and they wanted a better look. The three girls snuck quietly to the base of the huge oak in which the boys had built the tree house, and then one at a time, the girls climbed the ladder which leaned against the tree. Janet was the last one to start climbing the ladder and when she went to step on the third rung, her foot slipped and she let out a little yelp!

Instantly, the door to the tree house swung open and her two older brothers came rushing out, faces red, and fists in the air, ready to swing at the intruders. All three girls jumped off their place on the ladder and hurried out to the barn where they expected their father to intervene. The girls entered the barn just minutes before the boys caught up to them. Before their father could assess the situation and step in, the boys started pummeling their sisters. All three girls cried out in pain and fear but their brothers were not deterred; if anything, they seemed more energized by their sister's cries.

Janet's father didn't know why the boys were so angry but he knew they were being unreasonably harsh with the girls so he stepped into the melee and pulled Janet's two sisters to safety. He led them from the barn and disappeared with them, leaving Janet to fend for herself as both brothers now vented their anger on her. When the boys finally felt vindicated, they left the barn with a final warning that things would be much worse if she ever went near their tree house again.

Janet nursed her physical wounds with a disinfectant and bandages but she didn't know how to nurse her emotional wounds. She was hurt by her brother's fierce anger and beating, but she was even more deeply hurt by the fact that her father had protected her sisters but left her to fend for herself.

Later, Janet asked her father why he hadn't come back to rescue her. He replied, "Because you're not a girl; you can take care of yourself." Then he turned and walked out of the room with a smirk on his face. Janet looked down at her bruised arms and wondered what part of her was not a girl.

Janet was ten years old when this happened; today she is thirty-four but she cannot put this incident and many similar ones out of her mind. Janet's thoughts take her back daily to thoughts of her childhood and the abuse and neglect she experienced from her father. Over and over, Janet relived the abusive incidents, remembering every word, every inflection of the words, every look on her father's face, and every feeling she had felt at the time.

One day, as Janet was reliving one of the abusive incidents, she realized that she felt much the same today as she had felt as a ten year old. She still felt unworthy to be loved; she still felt unworthy to be a wife and mother, and in fact, she still felt that no one would want to be her friend.

As a result, Janet isolated herself as a way of protecting herself from being rejected by others. She had been asked out on many dates as a teenager and young adult, but she had never accepted that any man would ever love her so she had rejected all of her boyfriends before they could reject her. At thirty-four, Janet was living alone and spending long hours at her job as an accountant. She rarely went out and when she did, she would go to the opera or the movies, places where she would not be required to talk to anyone.

In all of this, Janet didn't blame her father; instead, she felt that she must have done something to deserve his abusive treatment.

*   *   *

Understanding that the Bible wants us to have a healthy self esteem is the first step to developing this healthy self view. Secondly, we need to recognize that our thoughts, our attitudes, and our emotions influence our self-esteem. Let's look in more detail at the importance of our thought life and its effect on assertiveness, and vice versa, how assertiveness can change our thought life.

Dr. David Burns, in his book, <u>Feeling Good</u>, (p.4) says that all of our moods come from our thought life, and we know that our thoughts and moods lead to our actions. If we are not assertive, we will believe that we have no control over our thoughts and that we simply need to accept our thoughts and the feelings they generate.

An assertive person will realize that we have the power to control our thoughts. When we recognize that we are thinking negative thoughts, we need to take control, put away those negative thoughts and foster more positive thoughts.

Everyone has thoughts, they are an integral part of us, and they can influence us in numerous ways. In a poem called, **I AM YOUR MASTER!** our thoughts are described as powerful, and working either for us, or against us. The poem ends with these thought provoking words, "I can never be removed…only replaced." It is important that we refuse to let our thoughts master us; instead, we need to recognize whether our thoughts are working for us or against us, then choose to replace those thoughts that are working against us.

God knows that how we think will affect our moods, words and actions. In fact, our thought life affects our self-esteem and our character. We can see this from Proverbs 23:7, "For as he thinks in his heart, so is he:" Since our thought life produces our character; we can change our character by changing our thoughts. Romans 12:2a in the NIV says, "Do not conform any longer to the pattern of this world, but be transformed by the renewing of your mind." We can choose the kind of thoughts that we want to think. Our minds can be likened to a garden in which we plant seeds. If we want to produce a healthy character, it is our responsibility to plant good, healthy seeds that will produce good fruit, known as positive feelings and actions. If we do not plant good seeds/thoughts in our minds, negative thoughts/weeds will plant themselves. As the poem says, our thoughts can never be removed, only replaced.

Our mind does not know the difference between the truth and a lie; it will function on the thoughts it is fed. Therefore, we need to confront our negative thinking and begin to focus on positive thoughts.

One of the ways that we can confront our thinking is through self-talk. Self-talk refers to the things we say to ourselves; since it is done silently for the most part, it is really just another form of thinking.

The things we say to ourselves are powerful. We will respond just as strongly to our self-talk as we would respond to the words of another person. If someone criticizes us, we feel badly about it, but how often do we criticize ourselves, and think we deserve it? It is important to be realistic and admit when we have made mistakes and seek to correct our behavior; however, many times we are unjustly harsh with ourselves. If our negative self-talk has such a powerful effect on us, then it is reasonable to assume that positive self-talk will also have a strong impact on us. We need to consciously change our self-talk to be positive, as soon as we recognize that we are indulging in negative self-talk.

In the counseling office, we have the opportunity to challenge our clients to change their thinking, and as a result, their behavior. Often they will indicate that they can't help their thinking or their actions when they are upset. To challenge their thinking, we may ask, "If someone offered you a million dollars to make better choices, do you think you could do it?" Or we might ask them, "Suppose your pastor or your mother was standing beside you, could you make better choices?" Almost always, they will sheepishly answer, "I guess I could."

If we are successful in getting clients to think more positively, we also see positive changes in the way they feel about themselves and in the way they behave.

Someone has said, "You can't stop a bird from flying over your head, but you can stop it from building a nest in your hair."

I, Martha, strongly believe that we can be in control of our thinking and self-talk. I am as human as anyone, and I have experienced occasions where I have had feelings of sadness or regret. I have learned not to give in to those feelings without questioning their validity. When I have realized that I was feeling sad, I tried to determine what thoughts had caused those feelings. At times I couldn't remember what I might have been thinking, so I simply looked for any evidence for why I should be feeling sad. If there was no evidence, I determined to put away those negative feelings and thank God for my blessings. These happy thoughts soon led to happier feelings.

Of course there will be times when we experience legitimate feelings of sadness caused by a loss; it is important not to push these sad thoughts aside. If we have lost a loved one, or even a job or a pet; we need to give adequate time to our grieving. Pushing away sad thoughts at those times may be an attempt at denial; it is important to be in touch with our feelings, face those feelings, grieve, and then move forward. Even when we have mostly healed from our grief and have moved on, we need to be aware that sad feelings could come back suddenly and unexpectedly. When they do, we need to pay attention, then use some self-talk to move forward once again.

If we are experiencing feelings of regret due to the fact that we have done something which has caused someone to be harmed in any way, we need to apologize to that person and make amends when necessary. It is an assertive, courageous act to admit to someone that we have wronged them, and to ask for their forgiveness.

Many times there is no reason why we should feel sad or regretful; at those times we need to use self-talk to put those feelings aside and focus on more positive thoughts. It is important to always focus on the fact that God is for us, not against us. God knows that often, "… the thoughts of man…are futile." Psalm 94:11 NKJV. God wants us to take control of our thoughts to change them into positive thoughts that will help us to enjoy our lives and to bless others.

SELF-TALK IN THE BIBLE:

The Bible also gives us examples of self-talk. David, in Psalm 42:5 gives us a really good example of how positive self-talk helps us to face challenging times. He says, "Why are you cast down, o my soul? And why are you disquieted within me? Hope in God, for I shall yet praise Him for the help of His countenance." After challenging himself to be hopeful, David talks to God, admitting that his soul is cast down but assuring God that he will remember the goodness of God in times past which gives him hope for the future. Then in verse 11, David repeats the exercise of positive self-talk, once again reminding himself to hope in God, knowing he will be able to praise Him for His help.

Unfortunately, positive self-talk may give us the false illusion that all is well when we base it on something, or someone, other than God. This was the case with the rich man we read about in Luke 12. God called this man a fool because he put his trust in the earthly wealth he had stored up in his new barns, instead of in God. We read his positive self-talk in verse 19, "And I'll sit back and say to myself, My friend, you have enough stored away for years to come. Now take it easy! Eat, drink, and be merry!" Unfortunately, he did not have a relationship with God, and he died that night, having stored up earthly goods but having failed to prepare for eternity. In verse 21 we read, "Yes, a person is a fool to store up earthly wealth but not have a rich relationship with God."

From these two examples in Scripture we can see that it is not enough to be positive in our self-talk, it is also important that we base it on God, what He has done for us in the past giving us hope for what He will do for us in the future. It is important to acknowledge that it is God Who gives us the skills, abilities and courage to take on new challenges.

It is sad that most of the time our self-talk is negative, berating ourselves for something we have done, or even for who we are. So it is important to stop those negative thoughts, but how do we do that? II Corinthians 10:5b says we can do this by, "...bringing into captivity every thought to the obedience of Christ." When we realize we are giving in to the negative thoughts, we need to replace the negative thoughts with positive thoughts like Philippians 4:8 tells us, "Finally, brethren, whatsoever things are true, whatsoever things are honest, whatsoever things are just, whatsoever things are pure, whatsoever things are lovely, whatsoever things are of good report; if there be any virtue, and if there be any praise, think on these things." When we focus on the blessings we receive every day and begin to praise God for them, the negative thoughts will soon fade away.

Another way of taking the negative thoughts captive is to replace them with thoughts about others who may need our help in some way. When we realize that we have the power to bless others and we begin to do something to help those people, it takes the focus off of ourselves. In the end we feel better about ourselves too because we have been able to help someone else.

The passive person does not realize that they have the power to control their thoughts; passive people give in to their negative thoughts about themselves and others. They will often spend sleepless nights, nurturing critical thoughts and indulging in self pity. Sometimes clients have convinced themselves that nobody loves them and they nurture these thoughts to such a degree that they end up feeling suicidal.

Dr. David Burns in his book, <u>Feeling Good</u>, says that when others criticize us, it will only hurt us, if we believe that what they are saying is true. Again, we will only enjoy compliments if we believe the compliment is true. Passive people want to hear positive compliments, but they are not easily convinced about their legitimacy. Passive people also believe that other people are better; when they compare themselves with others, they always come up short. As a result, they struggle with self-consciousness and anxiety.

For this reason each one of us needs to say along with the Psalmist, "Search me, O God, and know my heart; Try me, and know my thoughts; And see if there be any wicked way in me, And lead me in the way everlasting." Psalm 139:23,24 KJV.

Our wicked ways had their origin in our thought life as confirmed by Matthew 15:19, "For out of the heart proceed evil thoughts, murders, adulteries, ..." As we grow in maturity and in our Christian lives, we need to change our thought life and say along with the writer of I Corinthians 13:11, "When I was a child, I spoke as a child, I understood as a child, I thought as a child; but when I became a man, I put away childish things."

* * *

This was certainly true for Louise; she just assumed that Tom was more important than she was and that he was more intelligent and better informed about everything than she was. Since she thought her ideas were not very important, she often kept quiet during group discussions in their Bible Study group, listening to what everyone else was saying. When she did venture to give her opinion about a certain topic, she quickly backed down if someone challenged her ideas. When she made a suggestion to Tom, he would usually ridicule her idea, and again, she would back down.

Being passive, Louise was often taken advantage of, and as a result, she spent a lot of time thinking about the hurtful things other people had done to her. She nurtured critical thoughts and felt very sorry for herself, spending many a night, tossing and turning, not able to sleep. Psalm 63:6 encourages us to, "... meditate on thee in the night watches.". If Louise and you and I will heed this Scripture, we will get the rest we all need and be able to wake the next morning feeling rested and looking forward to a new day.

Like a typical passive person, Louise was quick to blame herself when something went wrong; she kept wondering what she could have done wrong to cause Tom to be so upset with her, ending in their separation.

* * *

Monica realized the importance of believing what the Scriptures say about us; she knew it was important for her thoughts to be positive, yet realistic. Because of her past, Monica often found herself thinking negatively about herself. How could she be positive about herself when she felt so bad about abandoning her sister Julie, and especially for allowing herself to be tricked into prostitution? However, if she was going to think like God wanted her to think, she would need to make some changes. First of all, she would need to accept God's forgiveness for past mistakes and rejoice that He saw her as clean.

As a new person in Christ, Monica tried to be aware of her thoughts, and when she noticed they were negative, she determined to take those thoughts captive and focus on something positive. She no longer allowed negative or critical thoughts about others to keep her from a deep sleep. At times, she recognized that she needed to address an issue with someone so she made a plan to do so; then put it to rest for the night.

Monica began to believe that her ideas were as valid as those of other people so she did not hesitate to share ideas in a group setting. If someone challenged her idea, she did not feel threatened; if she felt strongly about her idea, she stood her ground while allowing that the other person had the right to their ideas.

In many ways, Monica was becoming an assertive person.

* * *

Jack and Tom thought alike in that they were both quick to blame everyone except themselves, when something went wrong. This was due to their tendency to be mostly aggressive in the way they interacted with others. Jack truly believed that he was only doing his duty when he sharply reprimanded some of his co-workers, and Tom was quick to agree with Louise that she was to blame for the disintegration of their marriage.

* * *

Samantha's thoughts were filled with selfish thoughts of what new item she could buy, or which party she could attend. She didn't take much time to think about how she could be a help to her mother, or how she could reach out to others. Being a teenager, Samantha wasn't mature enough to try to see where she had been wrong in situations; rather she blamed her mother or other adults, and she easily held grudges. These are tendencies of people who are passive/aggressive.

* * *

Both aggressive and passive/aggressive people tend to blame others. By doing so, it reveals their immaturity and it goes against what God wants of us. Isaiah 58:9 (NIV) says, "Then you will call and the Lord will answer; ... **if** you do away with the yoke of oppression, with the pointing finger and malicious talk." The word "if" implies that God puts a condition on answering our prayers; that condition is to stop blaming others and talking maliciously about them

Chapter III

HOW OUR ATTITUDES AFFECT
OUR SELF-ESTEEM

We had not seen Cori Graham (not her real name), for some time. She was a journalist working for a national television station, reporting from Afghanistan. Although we had not see her reports for some time, we didn't realize that Cori was in trouble. The television station kept the news of Cori's kidnapping quiet and asked all other television stations to do the same. They did not want to give the terrorists any air time which is what they likely wanted, thinking it would improve their chances of collecting a big ransom.

In the end, Cori was released by her captors and we were able to hear about her terrifying experience through the many interviews which she gave at that time. It was very obvious that Cori's positive attitude contributed a lot to her eventual release.

Cori was seized at gunpoint and when she resisted her kidnappers, she was stabbed in her shoulder. Perhaps she passed out momentarily, but the next thing she knew, she was on the floor of the back seat of the kidnapper's vehicle. After a harrowing trip in this position, the car finally came to a stop in a place that looked completely unfamiliar to the journalist.

Instead of begging for mercy, Cori kept demanding that her kidnappers tell her where they were taking her. They didn't tell her, but when they arrived at their destination, they pointed to a small hole in the ground, telling her that's where she would be held. Again she showed her courage and told them she would never get in the hole; she would sleep outside instead. She didn't have any choice in the matter when one of the kidnappers picked up her tiny body and threw it into the hole. After getting herself oriented, she discovered that there was a short tunnel leading to a somewhat larger hole than the one into which she had first been dropped. However, the space in which she ended up staying was still very small.

Cori ended up in captivity for twenty-eight days and she could easily have slipped into despair of ever being rescued but she did not allow herself to do this. Instead, she determined that she would not die in this hole; dying was simply not an option. She kept assuring herself that help was on the way, that the people she worked for were hard at work negotiating her release.

She spent a fair bit of time with one of her kidnappers and even interviewed him. After all, she was a journalist; that is what she did. To further pass the time and to keep her sanity, she wrote letters to her friends, documenting the details of her captivity. When she was finally released, her body was weak and tired but her spirit remained strong. I believe she would credit her faith in God and her positive attitude for helping her to survive this horrible ordeal.

* * *

The attitudes we entertain make a huge difference in how much we enjoy life. It is very important to be aware that what happens to us is not as important as how we respond to those things. A positive attitude will help us get through a lot of difficult things in life.

In his book, <u>Man's Search for Meaning,</u> Viktor E. Frankl who was imprisoned during World War I, and who lost his family and everything that was important to him, says that, "everything can be taken from a man but one thing: the last of the human freedoms – to choose one's attitude in any given set of circumstances, to choose one's own way." P.104. We do indeed, have the freedom to choose our attitude in any situation we find ourselves. When we choose a positive attitude regardless of how difficult our situation may be, we will be able to get through it more successfully.

Our attitudes are affected by what we learned as a child. Clients often come into our office, vowing that they will not be like one, or both, of their parents. When we do some testing, we often find that they are repeating exactly what their parents did and they have the same negative attitudes.

Why does this happen? When we focus so strongly on what we want to avoid, we are simply reinforcing the negative, and we become what we think about. Our goal should be to have a new way of thinking which will lead to more positive attitudes.

In John 5:19 NIV it says, "...the Son can do nothing by himself, he can only do what he sees his Father doing, because whatever the Father does the Son also does." Jesus is talking about Himself, but since we are also sons and daughters of God as Christians, we should try to imitate our heavenly Father as Jesus did.

A few years ago, a little bracelet with the letters WWJD became popular; the letters stood for the question, "What would Jesus do?" This should be our new goal, not to avoid being like our earthly parents, but seeking to be like our heavenly Father and like Jesus. If we focus on this, we will have a positive attitude.

The important thing to remember is that we can change our attitudes when we change our thinking. The well-known poem called **A STATE OF MIND**, confirms the importance of a positive attitude.

A STATE OF MIND

Anonymous
If you think you are beaten, you are;
If you think you dare not, you don't.
If you like to win, but think you can't,
It's almost a cinch you won't.

If you think you'll lose, you're lost;
For out in the world we find
Success begins with a fellow's will;
It's all in the state of mind.
For many a game is lost
Ere even a play is run,
And many a coward fails
Ere even his work is begun.

Think big and your deeds will grow,
Think small and you'll fall behind,
Think that you can and you will
It's all a state of mind.

If you think you are outclassed, you are;
You've got to think high to rise,
You've got to be sure of yourself
Before you can win the prize.

Life's battles don't always go
To the stronger or the faster man;
But sooner or later the man who wins
Is the man who thinks he can.

Let me remind you once again, that with regard to our attitude, it is important to remember that what happens to us is not as important as how we respond to those things. This is where we see a big difference in the four personality types.

When something bad happens to us...

The passive person, who feels like a victim, will feel sorry for himself about what has happened.

The aggressive person will experience anger and blame, and will try to get revenge on whoever might be responsible.

The passive/aggressive person will feel that he doesn't deserve this treatment and he will try to hurt the other person in a devious, underhanded way.

The assertive person will look at what happened, allow himself to acknowledge negative feelings, decide what action needs to take place, and do it. If nothing can be done, he will adjust his attitude to accept what happened, and determine to make the best of it.

Some time ago, we came across this short article on attitude in a little brochure, with no name attached as the author. It reads as follows:

> "The longer I live, the more I realize the impact that attitude has on my life.
>
> Attitude is more important than facts.

It is more important than education, than money, than circumstances, than failures, than successes, than what other people think or say or do.

It is more important than appearance, giftedness or skills. It will make or break a company or a home.

The remarkable thing is we have a choice every day regarding the attitude we will embrace for that day. We cannot change the fact that people will act in a certain way. We cannot change the inevitable. The only thing we can do is play on the one string we have, and that is our attitude.

I am convinced that life is 10% what happens to me and 90% how I react to it.

And so it is with you...we are in charge of our attitudes."

THE BIBLE ON ATTITUDE:

The Bible has a lot to say about our attitudes. Jesus is our example of someone having an attitude of humility. Philippians 2:3-4 encourages us "Let nothing be done through selfish ambition or conceit, but in lowliness of mind let each esteem others better than himself. Let each of you look out not only for his own interests, but also for the interests of others."

One very important way in which we can look out for the interests of others is to encourage them. We use Hebrews 3:13 as our theme verse for the counseling office; this verse exhorts us to "But encourage one another daily...so that none of you may be hardened by sin's deceitfulness."

We believe that everyone needs to receive encouragement; life is hard enough without criticizing others when they fail. They need to be encouraged that even though they have failed in some areas, God wants to forgive them and wants them to learn from their failures.

Often in our counseling office, we use illustrations about people like Thomas Edison who tried many times to invent the light bulb before he actually succeeded. Then there is Colonel Saunders who was sixty before he succeeded in business with his Kentucky Fried Chicken. We could name many other people who failed numerous times before they were successful. We like to tell clients that the only real failure is the failure to keep on trying.

Back in Philippians 2:5-8 we read, "Let this mind be in you which was also in Christ Jesus, who, being in the form of God, did not consider it robbery to be equal with God, but made Himself of no reputation, taking the form of a bondservant, and coming in the likeness of men. And being found in appearance as a man, he humbled Himself and became obedient to the point of death, even the death of the cross." To have the same mind which was in Christ Jesus means that we are to be humble, willing to put others first and willing to do menial tasks which others may not be willing to do.

In Colossians 3:12 we are encouraged, "...as the elect of God, holy and beloved, put on tender mercies, kindness, humility, meekness, longsuffering;..." The attitude of humility is very important in the life of the assertive person because there will be times when he will offend someone else, and he will need to go to that person to make amends. This will take humility and courage.

By looking at the Bible, we can see that a balanced approach is what God wants for us; our attitude is to be one of humility, yet having a healthy self-esteem and a willingness to reach out to others in Christian love.

Assertive people focus on solutions while non-assertive people focus on the problems. Joseph in the Bible demonstrated this attitude of focusing on solutions. He was sold into slavery by his brothers where he encountered many problems. The Pharaoh who owned him was married to a beautiful woman who tried to seduce Joseph. When he refused to yield to her seduction, she cried "rape" which resulted in Joseph being thrown into prison. Joseph could have sulked in a corner, reviewing in his mind how unfair it had been of his brothers to sell him into slavery and how very unfair it had been of his master's wife to accuse him falsely. Instead, Joseph showed himself to be a responsible man who was soon given the responsibility of being in charge of the prison.

During his time in prison he interpreted the dreams of the butler and the baker; the butler was restored to his position of serving his master while the baker met his Maker in death. Joseph had accurately interpreted their dreams. When the butler was released from prison, Joseph asked him to put in a good word for him with his master. But the butler, now content in his former position, forgot all about Joseph until two years later when Pharaoh had a dream which needed interpretation. When his wise men were unable to interpret the dream the butler's memory was triggered and he recounted to his master how Joseph had correctly interpreted his dream while in prison.

Joseph was released from the prison and brought before Pharaoh where he was asked to interpret his dream. Joseph made it very clear that it was God who gave him the interpretation, then proceeded to give the interpretation to his master. Joseph did not return to prison, rather, he was given the responsibility of overseeing the preparations for the coming famine which the dream had predicted.

When Joseph's brothers came to Egypt to buy grain, he recognized them. When he revealed himself to his brothers after some initial testing, they were frightened; sure that Joseph would seek his revenge. Instead, Joseph assured his brothers, "As far as I am concerned, God turned into good what you meant for evil." Genesis 50:20a NLT. Joseph didn't waste precious time sulking or feeling sorry for himself, nor did he plot revenge, filled with resentment. He was sure that God could and would, turn his troubles into something good, and God did!

Wes and I have also experienced some difficult situations, although not as traumatic as that experienced by Joseph. It was 1990 when we had invested a lot of time, effort and money into a project which should have given us good returns. Then, because of some unfair business transactions by others, we lost our home and everything we owned except for an old 1978 Cougar, some used furniture, and $2,000.00.

We were very hurt and disappointed. However, God gave us some special verses from Habakkuk 3:17,18 at the time, "Though the fig tree does not bud and there are no grapes on the vines, though the olive crop fails and the fields produce no food, though there are no sheep in the pen and no cattle in the stalls, <u>yet I will rejoice in the Lord, I will be joyful in God my Savior. The Sovereign Lord is my strength; he makes my feet like the feet of a deer, he enables me to go on the heights.</u>"

God had proven Himself trustworthy in the past and we were not about to lose hope in Him now. We determined to rejoice in the Lord and trust that He would provide for us. We loaded our few possessions on a small moving truck, drove the old Cougar to another province, and with part of the $2,000.00 paid a deposit on a condo that we rented.

Life was not easy for a number of years, but God always provided what we really needed. At this point, God has showered us with bountiful blessings, and we couldn't be more content in our new home, city and province. It's very possible that without this difficult time, we may never have found our new home where God has blessed us with family, friends, church, and our counseling office.

We're not trying to say that if you always have the right attitude, you will be rewarded with ease for the rest of your life. What we are saying, is that because God helped us to have a positive attitude, we didn't waste precious time harboring resentment against the people who hurt us, and we were able to move ahead without bitterness blocking our path. We did experience angry feelings but we worked through them, and continued to trust God to show us His plan in all of this.

Assertive people recognize that having an attitude of gratitude is one of the ways that we can focus on solutions rather than on the problems. A passive person finds it very difficult to let go of the past and they will also worry excessively about the future. An aggressive person tries to get revenge on those who have caused his problems; when he is unable to get this revenge, he will often spew his anger on anyone who might be in his path.

This attitude of gratitude is not something that we are encouraged to have in our country where we have more than enough. Instead, we are bombarded with commercials that try to convince us that we need even more. The result is that we whine about the things we do have instead of being thankful that we have so much.

We find that often our clients will compare themselves with others and come up short with regard to appearance, performance, or importance. We will encourage these clients that God sees their value just because He created them; they do not need to compare themselves to someone else but accept God's evaluation of them.

The only time we should compare ourselves with others is in order to realize how much we have to be thankful for, not only at Thanksgiving. In an email someone sent to us, we are asked to compare ourselves with people living in third world countries and realize that we have good government on the whole; we have enough food to eat so that we never need go to bed hungry; we can go to the nearest department store to buy a new pair of shoes when we have outgrown ours; and we don't need to look over our shoulder when we walk down the street, expecting a terrorist attack at any moment. There are many more things for which we should be thankful. We could all benefit from making a plan to keep a "Gratitude" journal; if we wrote down even three things that we are thankful for each day, our attitude might soon be one of gratitude rather than discontent.

LIVE IN THE MOMENT:

A final thought in this section deals with the fact that many of us miss out on enjoying what we are experiencing **in the moment**; instead we harbor and relive regrets from the **past**, or we have apprehension about the **future**. When we allow our past to damage our self-esteem by continuing to regret those actions that caused pain for ourselves or others, we are not accepting God's forgiveness. Perhaps we are holding onto pain that others have caused. If so, we are not willing to forgive them for these actions and that only causes more pain, not for our offenders, but for us. Either way, we are not enjoying the present when we hang onto the past and this in turn, can lead to self-hatred instead of a healthy self-esteem.

Feeling apprehensive about the future robs us of present joy as well. In our worrisome thoughts we might envision a future scenario which is most unpleasant. Why would we want to experience unpleasant thoughts instead of enjoying the pleasure of the day? Some clients actually tell us their parents taught them to prepare for the worst so that if "the worst" doesn't happen, they will be pleasantly surprised. This is not good advice; save all your energies for meeting an actual crisis. That is not to say that we should envision a crisis-free future; we need to be prepared that life is bound to present us with challenges. However, that is not the same as expecting the very worst to happen in every situation.

When you think about future events, envision yourself talking and acting in ways that will help you to feel good about yourself. Prepare yourself to act in positive ways which will give you more confidence when you are in that future situation. And finally, remember that God will be with you in that future so we don't need to feel apprehensive about it. Enjoy today, even right NOW!

* * *

Monica had certainly struggled with her self-esteem. She was ashamed to let many people know about her family and all the negative things that had happened in her life. Twenty-one years earlier she had been born to parents who hardly knew she existed. She had grown up in this very dysfunctional home with parents who partied and used drugs in their own home, exposing the children to the fumes.

Monica had a younger sister, Julie, who was often left to fend for herself while she was at school and their parents were high on drugs. Many times when Monica would come home from school she would find Julie, who was only two years old, wearing the same diaper she had had on in the morning, and chewing on some moldy crackers she had found in the cupboard. Although she was only six years old herself, she would change Julie's diaper and get her some cereal for dinner.

Monica not only cared for her sister, but she was always trying to please her parents, hoping for their approval. But Monica never received her parents' approval so she thought there was something inherently bad about herself. Her experience after running away from home did nothing to counteract those feelings.

However as she learned more about God's love and how He viewed her, she was slowly learning to accept that she was someone to be valued and cared for.

Monica found that when she acted assertively in standing up for herself, her self-esteem blossomed, and the more she felt good about herself, the more easily she could stand up for herself.

Chapter IV

HOW OUR EMOTIONS AFFECT
OUR SELF-ESTEEM

Sally looked up when she heard the front door slam and was surprised to see her husband Roland, enter the house, his face red with anger. She wondered what she had done this time! Sally had learned not to cross Roland when he was angry and she knew this was one of those times. Roland's tall frame filled the doorway of the kitchen as he leaned forward, putting his face close to Sally's face, and with a snarl in his voice, he asked her why her car was sitting in the driveway instead of in the garage. Sally had planned to run to the grocery store for a few more groceries for a special treat she had planned for dinner later. When she tried to explain this to Roland, he growled, "A likely story! You just don't take care of that car! You're just lucky you get to use that car! I bet your friends don't get to drive such expensive cars!"

Sally cringed before her husband and tried to duck under his arm to leave the kitchen. Roland's arm swung down and caught Sally's shoulder hard so that she staggered back. Quickly, she turned and went into the living room. Roland followed her, screaming obscenities at her and calling her every name in the book!

Sally prayed silently and hoped that Roland would settle down soon and leave her alone. But Roland was not ready to end his tirade; he continued to follow Sally from room to room, shouting all the while. Seeing her husband wouldn't leave her alone, Sally stopped suddenly, turned around and demanded, "Why don't you just hit me and get it over with?!" Caught off guard, Roland stared at Sally, spit in her face, and left the house.

Sally knew he would not be home again until late. When he would come in, he would probably be full of remorse and she would have to deal with trying to assure him of her forgiveness. She sighed, went to wash her face in the bathroom, and started dinner without the extra groceries. There would be no special treat for dessert tonight!

* * *

In the same way that we can choose our attitude, we can also choose our emotions. As we have said earlier, our thought life leads to our moods; therefore, if our moods or emotions are negative, we probably need to change our thoughts.

In Ephesians 4:22-24 we read, "...put off, concerning your former conduct, the old man which grows corrupt according to the deceitful lusts, and be renewed in the spirit of your mind, and (that you) put on the new man which was created according to God, in true righteousness and holiness."

Changing our thoughts will lead to healthier emotions but there will still be times when our emotions will seem to take over our thoughts and attitudes. At those times we need to be very aware of what is happening and make a thoughtful decision about how we will handle these emotions. As we practice thinking through things in a logical way, we can choose to feel differently; now our feelings or emotions will influence our words and actions in positive ways. It is impossible to be happy and cheerful all the time; there are legitimate times to feel sad, disappointed, fearful, or even angry. At these times we need to control our emotions instead of letting them control us.

Of all the emotions we experience, anger seems to give us the most trouble; Roland was a very angry man and he had not learned to control it.

Part of the reason anger gives us so much trouble is because it has been so misunderstood. Many of the clients who come to our office have been told by their parents or others that God doesn't want us to be angry, that it is sin. This is a misunderstanding; in Ephesians 4:26 we read, "Be ye angry, and sin not." Anger, in and of itself, is not wrong. In one of the best treatments on the topic of anger, <u>Make Anger Your Ally,</u> Neil Warren says,

> "… anger is simply a state of physical readiness. When we are angry, we are prepared to act. Anger is simply preparedness.
>
> The value of anger is determined by how it is expressed. It can be used to make things right or to destroy everything and everyone in sight. How anger is used is independent of what anger is."p.5,6

It is true that many of us use our anger in destructive, hurtful ways when we act on our anger before deciding how we want to use our anger. In God's Word we read, "…always be willing to listen and slow to speak. Do not become angry easily, because anger will not help you live the right kind of life God wants." James 1:19 NCV. In this verse, God gives us a formula for dealing with our anger.

When we carefully visualize what's happening in this verse, it's clear that at least two people are involved in an interaction with one another. We may be on the receiving end of hearing words that are causing us to move into that state of physical readiness that we call anger. Our natural impulse is to protect ourselves but we are advised that instead of giving in to quick anger, we should be quick to listen and slow to speak. Listening carefully to what our opponent is saying will help us to understand what he or she may be feeling; it is possible that they are reacting to a hurt that we have first inflicted on them. Or perhaps they are simply speaking out of pain in their life caused by others and they are letting this hurt and anger spill out on us. **We need to be willing to listen!**

Secondly, we are to be slow to speak; I believe that means we need to **think** carefully about what we will say when we do speak. We may want to say something like, "It sounds like you are really upset today; I'm sorry you feel that way. Let me see if I understand what you just said." Then we can use reflective communication to rephrase what they said. If they have accused us of something that we did not do, now that we have listened to them, we have won the right to tell them what happened from our perspective. **We need to think before we speak!**

And third, we are not to become angry easily because anger will not help us live the right kind of life that God wants us to live. I believe this is referring to easy anger that reacts quickly without taking time to listen or think; it is referring to anger that is controlling us and which results in abusive words or actions which we have not thought through carefully. This is not pleasing to God so the third point is **we need to control our anger!**

But how do we control our anger? I think the first thing we need to do is to ask ourselves why we are reacting in anger. If we have a poor self-esteem, we will be quick to defend ourselves and we are often angry in our defense. There may be other reasons why we feel angry; perhaps someone is expecting too much of us or perhaps someone is abusing our boundaries. If we can identify what is causing our anger, then we need to tell the other person in a firm, but calm manner, why we feel upset. Next we can ask for specific changes and tell them what the consequences will be if they do not make those changes.

In Ephesians 4:26 & 27 we are told, "When you are angry, do not sin, and be sure to stop being angry before the end of the day. Do not give the devil a way to defeat you." If we do not control the anger we feel, we will be giving the devil a way to defeat us. After we have hurt others by our words or actions, we will feel defeated in our desire to live lives pleasing to God. We cannot take back the words we have spoken or undo our actions; at best, we can apologize and ask for their forgiveness.

I believe that when God asks us to stop being angry before the end of the day, he wants us to talk about our anger with the other person and come to an agreement about who needs to do what to restore the relationship. This is very difficult for people who are not assertive. The passive person is much more likely to review what happened over and over in his mind for much of the night, preventing a good night's sleep. This is also giving the devil a foothold; he wants us to be upset and unforgiving. He wants to destroy relationships. The aggressive person will most often express his anger through abusive words or actions, and the passive/aggressive person will scheme how to get revenge, often in devious ways. Again, these are some ways that we can give the devil a foothold in our lives. The assertive person knows it takes courage to address issues with an offender, but they also know that unless they address the issue, the relationship may be in jeopardy and since they value relationships, they will do their best to deal with issues as they arise.

Neil Warren explains that there are many layers involved in the emotion of anger. Under the layer of raw anger, we may have layers of frustration, confusion, hurt and fear. Warren says that every time we feel anger our bodies are prepared to act; if we do not work through the feelings of anger to arrive at a state of contentment, we will continue to deal with a heightened state of agitation. To deal with our agitation we can choose to fight or flee.

Passive people will often direct their anger at themselves by taking the blame for the situation that caused their anger. Being too passive to confront the person who was actually to blame for the hurtful event, they find it easier to blame themselves and they may sink into a state of depression. This is one way of fleeing. An aggressive person will strike out, blaming others even when he is responsible for what happened. He will physically or verbally fight with the other person.

Warren agrees that our emotions and our self-esteem are inter-related:

> 'The more positively you view yourself, the less anger you experience. And the more effectively you handle your anger, the better you will feel about yourself…. That's the beauty of working on both your self-concept and your anger expertise at the same time. Any improvement in one immediately benefits the other. And when you get both of these systems moving at once, the momentum you can build leads to incredible growth." P.176

When we have a healthy self-esteem, we are able to use our anger in constructive ways to resolve conflicts in relationships and to work for change in our world that will benefit not only ourselves, but many others. With a healthy self-esteem, we will learn how to control our anger impulses. Pushing our anger down into our subconscious is not a healthy way of controlling our anger, nor is using aggression to hurt someone with our words or actions. Being devious and underhanded is definitely not how God would want us to deal with our anger.

A healthy way of dealing with our anger is to be very realistic about how we feel. We may need to step away from a situation and carefully evaluate what we will do about the situation which resulted in our anger. We need to realize that if we try to push our anger down into our sub-conscious, it will result in bitterness and resentment. Often, we spew out our unresolved anger on unsuspecting and undeserving people. In Hebrews 12:15 we read, "See to it that no one comes short of the grace of God; that no root of bitterness springing up causes trouble; and by it many be defiled;" From this we can conclude that stuffing our angry feelings is not the right way to control our anger.

Let's continue to examine our anger, remembering that according to Warren, there are many layers to our anger. We need to ask ourselves if our heightened state of preparedness is due to feeling hurt, frustrated, or threatened. If we can determine the cause of our anger, we will be able to recognize whether our anger is legitimate or if we are being overly sensitive. Often, we will realize that we are being too sensitive, that we should not take the incident personally, so we can let go of our angry feelings.

If however, we realize that we were treated unfairly and our anger is legitimate, then we need to decide how we will use our anger constructively. The first thing that can defuse some of our strong emotions is to journal about what happened and how it has caused us to feel frustrated, hurt or threatened. Sometimes we will feel all three of these emotions. Journaling defuses some of the strong feelings, which, if not acknowledged, could burn like acid in our stomachs.

Secondly, acknowledging our feelings about the anger-producing incident by journaling is one way of validating our feelings as being reasonable. When others tell us, "You shouldn't feel that way!", they are not validating us and we feel even worse. We need to feel validated, and when we have a healthy self-esteem, we will be confident to validate our own feelings. Of course the opposite could also happen; we could realize through journaling that we were being overly sensitive and we need to let go of those angry feelings.

Journaling about our feelings associated with our anger will also allow us to think through the incident in a logical way and prepare us for the next step which is to lovingly confront the person who hurt us. Ephesians 4:15 talks about "… speaking the truth in love…" which is loving confrontation with a goal to restore the relationship. In our counseling office, we often suggest that the first step in confrontation could be in the form of a letter. The letter should clearly spell out, using "I" messages, how the writer feels about what the other person did. He should indicate his desire to restore the relationship as well. If the person receiving the letter responds positively, the two will be able to meet face to face and work at forgiveness and reconciliation.

I heard author Paul Williams say in an interview, that "Forgiveness is really in the hands of the victim, but reconciliation is really in the hands of the perpetrator." This statement is verified in our office especially when we deal with sexual abuse victims. To receive healing, sexual abuse victims will need to forgive to be able to move on, but reconciliation will depend, to a large extent, on the response of the perpetrator. If there is any danger of further abuse, we do not recommend reconciliation; the victim's forgiveness can be completely genuine without reconciliation.

The assertive person will at times experience other negative emotions as well. When we experience guilt, shame or fear, we can use a similar formula to deal with our emotions. Rather than trying to downplay or stuff those emotions, the assertive person will seek to be in touch with his feelings, determine <u>what</u> he is feeling, ask himself <u>why</u> he is feeling this way, and finally, he will decide <u>what to do</u> about these feelings. Sometimes, he will decide to shift his focus and move on, but other times, action may be required to deal with these negative emotions. The important thing to note is that the assertive person will experience the positive emotions of love, joy and peace, more often than he experiences negative emotions.

The aggressive person deals with a lot of angry feelings; not having learned a positive way of dealing with those emotions, he will blame others as the cause of his anger, and strike out at them. Sometimes he will be verbally abusive and other times he will strike out to hurt others physically.

The passive/aggressive person experiences anger and will often hold grudges rather than seek to resolve the cause of his anger. In trying to get revenge on the person he is blaming, he will use deceitful methods so that he cannot be found responsible, things like gossip, sarcasm, giving someone the silent treatment, or bringing up old issues.

The passive person will feel anger but mostly they will feel sorry for themselves. They do not have the courage to address the issue with the person who offended them, so they keep it inside where they nurture it until it becomes bitterness and resentment.

The passive person allows the "Fear of man ... to be a snare,..." Proverbs 29:25. The NLT of Galatians 1:10 reads, "Obviously, I'm not trying to be a people pleaser! No, I am trying to please

God. If I were still trying to please people, I would not be God's servant."

One of the ways that this fear of man reveals itself is that we can become "people pleasers". We have witnessed many clients trying so hard to please others that they lose their own identity, not knowing who they really are, or want to be. We lose our own identity because we don't feel the freedom to think our own thoughts, feel our own emotions, or do what we really want to do. We are constantly wondering what someone else would want us to think, feel, or do in every situation in which we find ourselves.

This tendency to be a people pleaser is especially problematic when one spouse in a marriage tries to please parents over his or her spouse. This was the situation with Trent and Lorie. Trent's mother did not approve of his marriage to Lorie and after the wedding she continued to treat Lorie with distain; she hardly acknowledged her presence in the room when they were both at the same function. She also took it on herself to tell both Trent and Lorie how to raise their two girls, always assuring them that God had told her to help them in this way. It's hard to argue with someone who says they are only doing what God directed them to do. This can be spiritual abuse and we need to address it as such when we recognize it.

Trent and Lorie felt helpless to confront Trent's mother so she continued her controlling ways, interfering in their lives. After coming for several sessions of counseling and learning how to be assertive, Trent and Lorie were visiting at his parent's home when once again, Trent's mother started telling Trent what they were doing wrong as parents. Trent decided it was time to speak up, so while still trying to be respectful, he addressed his mother firmly. "Mom, you've never treated Lorie with respect; instead, you've acted as though she doesn't exist. This cannot go on; Lorie is my wife, she is a wonderful wife and a good mother to our children. From now on I want you to treat Lorie with respect or we will not be coming over. As for the parenting tips, if we ask you for advice, then you can give us some tips, if we don't ask, don't tell us what we're doing wrong. You and dad had a chance to raise us and you probably made some mistakes; you need to pray for us, but let us make our own mistakes."

At first Trent's mother became very defensive, trying to make excuses for what she had done. Thankfully, Trent's brother was also visiting his parents and he spoke up in Trent's defense, "Mom, you're not hearing Trent; please let him talk." Trent went on to explain to his mother how her treatment of his wife, and her interference in their parenting was causing marital problems between himself and Lorie. He took ownership of his failure to speak up sooner, and he asked her to allow them to make parenting decisions on their own. He assured her that they loved and respected her, but they also wanted her to respect them. Trent's mother wasn't ready to apologize but she grudgingly agreed to back off.

When Trent and Lorie drove back to their own home with the girls in the back seat, they felt like a huge stone had rolled off their shoulders. Lorie starting singing, "Rolled away, rolled away, rolled away, all the burdens of my heart rolled away." The girls joined them from the back and Trent reached out to squeeze Lorie's hand. She gave him a radiant smile and sang even louder. Both Trent and Lorie knew this was only a start. They would both have to continue being assertive with Trent's mother, respecting her knowledge and experience, but not allowing her to control their lives.

A passive, people-pleasing adult was very likely raised in a home where they were made to feel acceptable only if they behaved in ways that won their parents approval. Barbara Colorosa suggests that children who are reward-dependent will do what they are told to do without question, they lack initiative and wait for orders while feeling controlled at the same time. Due to bringing down the wrath of those in authority, they will hide their mistakes. When these characteristics continue to be part of a person's make-up, they will find it difficult to develop a healthy sense of self. (P. 65-66). When a child makes choices based on the rewards that have been promised, they have learned that it is safer to be and do what others want them to be and do, than to make choices that feel right for them. Consequently, these children have no sense of self because they cannot be true to themselves. They will likely grow up to be adults who find it very difficult to make decisions on their own, a characteristic which may well lead to problems in their relationships in marriage, with friends, and in the work place.

On the other hand, children who have developed a healthy self-esteem will demonstrate assertive characteristics like being able to make choices, take initiative without waiting for an adult's approval, and take ownership of their behavior and the consequences. They will see their mistakes as opportunities to learn from the past. These children will grow up to be capable, assertive adults who will make decisions based on what they believe is good for them and they will have less problems with relationships than non-assertive adults.

In her book, Colorosa quotes P.L. Cowan, "Mature self-esteem in adulthood is not a global capacity to feel good about oneself regardless of what transpires, but an ability to arrive at a realistic evaluation of the self after considering one's strengths, weaknesses, and life."

* * *

Monica struggled with her emotions; she often felt guilty and ashamed due to her dysfunctional background, and especially because of her experience at the "club"! . The morning that Monica decided to run away from home, she headed to the bus depot instead of the school; surely life would be better in another city. On the bus she met Randy who looked to be about eighteen; he seemed pleasant enough, and they soon got into an animated conversation.

When Randy found out that Monica was running away from home, he invited her to join him and some friends who were all sharing a rented house in a low-income district in the city they were heading to. Monica couldn't believe her luck; already things were looking up! When they arrived, Randy introduced Monica to his friends who welcomed her to their home; after all, one more person to help pay the rent would be useful. Monica looked for a job the next day, and the next, and the next, all without success! What would she do? She was expected to help with the rent, yet she couldn't find a job!

One day, Doug, the oldest resident of the house, came to Monica with a proposal. He suggested that if she couldn't find a job, perhaps she could do her share by coming to work at the club he belonged to downtown. Monica was so pleased that she didn't stop to ask what kind of work she would be required to do and the next day she was up bright and early, eager to go to her first job. Doug, however, was still sleeping. Monica waited patiently for him but he didn't emerge from his room until three in the afternoon!

Doug ate and dressed, and around four o'clock, Monica left with him in his fancy black car. She was excited about having work but it seemed strange that she would be starting so late in the day.

When they arrived at the club, Monica saw that it was a very plush club with soft chairs around small tables, and scantily dressed waitresses bringing drinks to the men who were lounging. She wondered what she would be asked to do in a place like this!

Monica didn't have to wait long to find out. Doug introduced her to his manager, who then took her up a long flight of stairs where he showed her into a room. The room had very little furniture, only a bed, a chair and a dresser. This did not feel right! The manager pointed to some lingerie set out on the bed and asked Monica to change into it. Then he told her that her first customer would be along soon and she would be expected to please him in whatever way he desired. When the manager had gone, Monica realized what was happening. How could she have been so blind! She looked for a way of escape; there was no place she could go, and when she tried the door, she found that it was locked!

Somehow, Monica got through the night and when she got into Doug's car to go back to the house early the next morning, she curled up into a little ball and tried to stifle her sobs. Doug told her to lighten up, that she would get used to it, and she would be able to make a lot of money.

When they arrived back at the house, Doug went immediately to his room. Monica did as well, but she had no intention of going to sleep or staying in this house any longer! Again she stuffed her belongings into her backpack, and when she was sure that Doug was asleep, she snuck out of the house.

Now, five years later, even though she had been duped into going along with Doug, she felt she should have known better. But after searching the Bible and listening carefully to the pastor's messages, Monica realized that God had completely forgiven all her past behavior and she no longer needed to feel guilty or ashamed.

Monica learned to accept God's forgiveness and was able to experience joy in her life. She still experienced negative emotions at times, but she made a real effort to be in touch with her feelings, and when she realized that she was being negative, she learned to ask herself four important questions: 1) What am I feeling? 2) Why am I feeling like this? 3) Is there any evidence for why I should be feeling like this? and 4) How do I want to feel? Having answered these questions, she was usually able to replace negative thoughts and emotions with more positive thoughts and soon she was feeling more positive about life.

* * *

Louise struggled a lot with guilt and shame, blaming herself, not only for the problems in her relationship with Tom, but also for the fact that she had never pursued her career of teaching, even though she had received her B.Ed. in college. She realized that Tom had not encouraged her to teach; he had always wanted her to be at home, ready to cater to his every need. Yet she felt that if she had been stronger, she could have followed her dream. Twenty-five years later, her certification was no longer valid.

Because Louise struggled with a defeatist attitude, and often second-guessed her own ideas, she felt that it was too late to try to upgrade her education, so she settled for remaining unemployed. She did think about looking for work as a waitress.

* * *

Pride and arrogance were the most common attitudes displayed by both Jack and Tom. They would never admit it, even to themselves, but often those attitudes were a cover-up for their own feelings of inadequacy.

Anger was their most common emotion, usually a result of someone questioning their authority on something. Neither tried to control their anger, but lashed out with mean words or even with physical force.

* * *

Immature attitudes of selfishness and seeking pleasure were the most common attitudes that Samantha experienced. She was happy when things went her way, but she was easily upset and angry when her plans were thwarted.

OUR SELF-ESTEEM AS A RESULT OF OUR THOUGHTS, ATTITUDES AND EMOTIONS:

Our thoughts, attitudes and emotions combine to form our self-esteem and self-view. Positive thoughts, attitudes and emotions will lead to a healthy self-esteem and self-view. Negative thoughts, attitudes and emotions will lead to a low self-esteem. Assertive people have a healthy self-esteem.

When we have a healthy self-esteem, we view ourselves as capable and able to defend ourselves if the need arises. We can also set healthy boundaries and address issues when someone has offended us.

With a healthy self-esteem, we are able to take responsibility for our actions, and admit when we have made a mistake. We are able to apologize and ask for forgiveness.

Assertive people try to see themselves the way God sees them, as worthy, valuable people, so much so, that God sent Jesus to die for them. As a result, they can go through life without a lot of anxiety or feelings of self-consciousness.

Overall, the assertive person has a healthy self-esteem, a balanced perspective where he seeks to see himself as God sees him, yet not in a position of power or status over others.

*John Burke says that the most harmful addiction we all suffer from is Self-Centeredness. Instead, we need to be God-Centered and Others-Centered. It may seem counter intuitive to suggest that when we have a healthy self-esteem, we are less Self-Centered than when we have a poor self-esteem. Having a low self-esteem keeps us focused on ourselves, always wondering what people are thinking of us, or feeling sorry for ourselves, or putting ourselves down. As an assertive person with a healthy self-esteem, we can feel confident that we are behaving in positive ways most of the time; instead of wasting time dwelling on how we are coming across, we can focus on how we can reach out to others and be aware of the promptings of God in our daily lives.

* * *

Louise's low self-esteem was evident in the way she put herself down and blamed herself for anything that went wrong. She never felt that she measured up to what was expected of her. This feeling had probably begun in her childhood when her parents, especially her father, were very demanding and constantly criticizing her when she failed to meet their expectations.

Marrying Tom only compounded her feelings of low self-esteem. Any time she had tried to assert herself in any way, Tom had put her down, and she gave up easily, believing she had no right to feel good about herself. She was a failure as a daughter, a wife, and even as a mother!

* * *

Jack believed he had a healthy self-esteem; however, his actions and words of bravado were really just a mask for his low self-esteem. He did not have the courage to apologize to his co-workers when they revealed how they had been hurt by his demanding, intimidating ways.

Jack also believed that in order to maintain his self-esteem, he needed to be in absolute control in his home. His wife and son were afraid of him and tried to please him to avoid his anger.

* * *

Samantha, as an immature teenager, thought she was a "princess" who needed pampering in her home and with her friends. Many of her girlfriends felt the same way, so she didn't always get the special treatment she was hoping for. At those times, she immediately struggled with her self-esteem and blamed others for her feelings.

Samantha's self-esteem could best be described as variable as the weather; when things were good, she felt good about herself but when things were not so good, her self-esteem plummeted.

* * *

Monica struggled with her self-esteem all the while that she lived at home. She was embarrassed by the behavior of her parents, by the poor quality clothing she was forced to wear to school, and by the dirty, unkempt condition of their home. Monica received no encouragement or affirmation from her parents even though she tried hard to please them. This led her to believe that she was unacceptable as a person. However, when Monica got involved in going to church with Mary, she heard and accepted the truth that God loves her and sees her as acceptable. She learned that she didn't need to be perfect before God would accept her even though some people still seemed to expect perfection from her. This was especially true when three weeks after leaving Doug, Monica realized that she was pregnant. By this time, she had found a job and was renting a cute little basement suite.

One morning, Monica shut off her alarm and jumped out of bed when a wave of nausea hit her. What was happening? She sank back down on the bed and tried to think. She knew that her period was late in coming, but she had thought it was only because of all the changes in her life. Now it dawned on Monica that she must have gotten pregnant during that night in the club. She was overwhelmed, what would she do? She called her friend Mary, after quickly leaving a message for her boss to say that she was sick and wouldn't be in. Mary promised she would come over as soon as she could, and suggested that the two of them should walk over to the church to talk to the pastor, and this time Monica agreed.

When Monica's pregnancy became evident to everyone, she felt judged by some people. This bothered her a lot, especially since she was really good at beating herself up without help from anyone. However, with time and learning more about God's unconditional love for her, Monica realized that the people who were judging her were in all likelihood struggling with their own lack of self acceptance. Monica made an effort to show them only kindness and acceptance and as she did, she felt more of God's love and acceptance. In the end she developed a mostly healthy self-esteem, only slipping into her old mindset on occasion.

Part III

ASSERTIVENESS IMPROVES
INTERPERSONAL RELATIONSHIPS

Chapter I

THE IMPORTANCE OF RELATIONSHIPS

Linda and Jason had dated for only three months when Jason popped the question. Linda was so thrilled that someone wanted to marry her, that she quickly said, "Yes!" She had noticed that Jason seemed really jealous when any other boys paid any attention to her but she shrugged it off as meaning that Jason loved her so much he was being a little possessive. He could be forgiven for that, after all, she wanted to know that he loved her more than anyone!

Linda wanted lots of time to plan the wedding but Jason was so anxious to get married that he talked Linda into setting the date only four months later. When Linda protested that she wouldn't have time to get ready, Jason claimed that if they waited, his best friend wouldn't be able to come. Jason said his friend was going to Japan for a year to teach English and he wanted his friend to be his best man. Linda relented, and with a lot of help from her mother and her girlfriends, everything was ready for the big day.

The wedding was beautiful and so much fun with all their favorite people attending. Soon it was time to leave on their honeymoon. Jason had everything arranged for their trip to a remote beachfront cabin about one hundred kilometers from their city. It was wonderful to have two whole weeks away; it was a good time to get to know each other better.

One evening Jason suggested to Linda that she could resign from her job when they got back home. Linda was shocked! They had never talked about this before; she enjoyed her job, and besides, they would need her income. But Jason was adamant; he claimed that if she continued to work, he would feel inadequate as a husband. Linda was disappointed but she wanted Jason to feel good about himself so she agreed.

Linda gave two weeks' notice at her job and on her last day of work, she went home feeling sad about leaving a job she enjoyed, and especially about leaving co-workers she considered friends. A little part of her also felt proud that her husband wanted to provide for her and pamper her.

With no job to fill her days, Linda suggested to Jason that this would be a good time for her to enroll in the pottery class she had always wanted to take. Jason didn't think that was a good idea. When Linda pushed him for a reason, he lamely suggested that they probably couldn't afford it now that she had quit her job.

Jason had already been living in his own house on an acreage ten kilometers from the city and this is where he moved his new bride. Now Linda, with no job, no opportunity to take up a hobby, and no friends nearby, soon succumbed to a mild depression. She tried to find pleasure in preparing special meals for her and Jason to enjoy when he returned home for dinner.

Jason usually questioned Linda carefully about her day. At first she thought he was just interested in her day, but one day he angrily accused her of going to the city during the day. She agreed that she had gone to the city to buy groceries and wondered why he was so upset. Jason replied, "Yes-s-s. And where else did you go?"

"What do you mean, Jason? I went for groceries and came straight home."

"Quit lying to me!" Jason shouted. "I know you've been sneaking around for some time now." "I've been checking the mileage on your car. If I catch you lying to me again, there will be trouble!"

Linda was shocked and hurt! Why would Jason accuse her of something she had not done? She knew she had driven a few extra blocks, trying to find a better parking spot, but that was all.

Soon Linda was aware that she could not go anywhere or do anything without being closely monitored by Jason. He not only checked the odometer on her car, he called her several times a day to make sure she was at home. If the T.V. or radio was playing in the background, he accused her of having company over.

Linda lived with Jason's possessive actions for many years, raising three wonderful children along the way. Jason became more and more paranoid about Linda's actions and even though she denied his accusations, Jason often beat her physically, just to "keep her from going astray".

Linda was so lonesome for relationships but there was not much she could do. When all three children had moved out, Linda realized she could no longer stay in this marriage. She feared for her life so one day she packed a suitcase, threw it into the trunk of her car, and headed for the city. Once there, she looked up the nearest women's shelter where she was received by compassionate women who helped her get some counseling. Eventually, Linda was able to file for divorce and regain the self-confidence to get a job and reconnect with many friends as well as make new friends.

* * *

Throughout our lives, we will be part of many different relationships. We are born into families, so we will always be in a relationship with parents and siblings. We will be in relationships with our peers at school and later with co-workers, and with the people that we choose to socialize with. We may be in dating relationships, and most of us will be in a marital relationship at some time in our lives.

Some of these relationships will be painful, but if we had to choose between risking some difficult relationships and spending our lives in isolation, I believe we would all risk difficult relationships. After all, why is the worst punishment for a prison inmate being put in solitary confinement?

John Burke, in his book, <u>Soul revolution</u>, says, "I've come to believe that our deepest longings only find fulfillment through relationships – with God and with other people. Without those relationships, our pursuits and goals and dreams and achievements are like that [toy] train going around in circles— what's the point?" p.10

Because relationships are so important, we need to know how to build and maintain healthy relationships. The Bible is our authority. When we look at the trinity, we see that God the Father, Jesus Christ the Son and the Holy Spirit are in constant relationship with one another and model healthy relationships for us. John 17:24 says that "… for You loved Me before the foundation of the world." Jesus was talking here about the love of the Father for Him. In the same way, there would have been love experienced between all three parts of the trinity.

One of the reasons there is perfect harmony in the relationships within the trinity is the fact that each person of the trinity has a specific role and no one tries to usurp the role of the others.

God, the Master Planner, said, "…Let us make man in our image, after our likeness: and let them have dominion over …" Genesis 1:26a KJV. When Adam and Eve sinned by listening to the serpent and eating the fruit which grew on the tree in the midst of the garden, God was not caught unawares. He had a plan to redeem mankind by sending His Son Jesus, to die for us, as announced in Genesis 3:15 NIV. In speaking to the serpent, God said, "'…I will put enmity between you and the woman, and between your offspring and hers; he will crush your head, and you will strike his heel.'"

Jesus, "… being in very nature God, did not consider equality with God something to be grasped, but made himself nothing, taking the very nature of a servant, …humbled himself and became obedient to death - even death on a cross!" Philippians 2:6-8. Jesus willingly took on the role the Father had planned for him. It is because Jesus was willing to live among mankind, and ultimately, to give His life for us, that we have the wonderful privilege of having a personal relationship with God the Father, Jesus Christ, and the Holy Spirit.

Much has been written about the sacrifice that Jesus made for us by taking on all of our sins as He hung on the cross and paid the debt that we should have paid. It is truly such an awesome sacrifice that our finite minds find it difficult to totally understand the gravity of what happened there. However, recently I have also begun to think more about the sacrifice that Jesus made by living among mankind. To be born in a humble stable to a young woman and to grow up in a carpenter's home was certainly a far cry from living with His Father. As a counselor, I am also aware that when He began

His ministry, He suffered not only physical abuse, but certainly verbal and psychological abuse. Some even feel that He suffered sexual abuse through hanging nearly naked, on the cross. This sounds reasonable to me, "For we do not have a high priest who cannot sympathize with our weaknesses, but One who has been tempted in all things as we are, yet without sin." Hebrews 4:15 NASV. Jesus continues in His role even now to be our "… mediator between God and men,…" I Timothy 2:5 NIV.

The Holy Spirit has many responsibilities. In John 16:7 the Holy Spirit is referred to as the Counselor and in verse 8 it lists some of His responsibilities: "When he comes, He will convict the world of guilt in regard to sin and righteousness and judgment. In verse 13 we read that "… he will guide you into all truth." And in verse 14 it mentions that He will bring glory to God instead of himself. Many other Scriptures assure us that the Holy Spirit is also our comforter.

When Jesus was on earth, He sought out a quiet place where He could spend time praying, connecting with His Father, and receiving guidance and encouragement. Jesus also spent a lot of time with His twelve disciples, teaching them how to follow Him and how to live with one another. I'd like to think that sometimes Jesus and the disciples simply sat around, discussing the events of the day, and shared some laughter and camaraderie. Author Paul Williams writes a wonderful book called The Shack, in which he describes in fiction, the delightful relationship between the Father, Son and Holy Spirit.

God created us for relationship with Him, but He also wants us to have healthy relationships with one another. In Romans 12:18 we are admonished, "If it is possible, as far as it depends on you, live at peace with everyone." But how do we do that? We believe the answer is assertiveness once again. If everyone applied the Golden Rule as well as the Silver Rule to their relationships, there would be more peace in our relationships.

I read a statement on a church sign recently which read, "Kindness is hard to give away, because it keeps coming back to you." That is another way of saying that if we treat others well, they will usually treat us well also. However, this does not always happen; some people are naturally nasty and feel the only way to get their own way is to be aggressive. This is when we need to apply the Silver Rule; instead of allowing others to treat us poorly, we need to address the issue, firmly but lovingly. There are many components which go into developing and maintaining healthy relationships; let's examine some of these.

Dr. Arnold and his wife Rachel, worked together in their medical clinic. Rachel was a nurse and had worked in hospitals for many years but when her husband opened his own clinic, she went to work for him. Two other doctors also shared the office space and they soon realized they needed more help with the filing and other office work.

Rachel contacted some of the local High Schools to see if the Guidance Counselor in each school might recommend a senior student who would really benefit from having a job, and who could be counted on to do a good job for them. Over the years a number of different girls worked for Dr. Arnold and Rachel. It was a good arrangement for everyone. Rachel was able to go home early to prepare dinner so that it was ready when Dr. Arnold came home and the girls who worked for them appreciated the work experience and the money they earned.

One day while opening the mail in the clinic, Rachel came across a letter from Karen, who had worked for them many years before. In the letter, Karen thanked Rachel and Dr. Arnold for the opportunity to work for them so many years ago. She told them that their confidence in her had really helped her self-esteem to blossom. The work experience had given her the motivation to pursue her chosen career, and overall, she was very grateful for their friendship.

Karen would agree with Proverbs 27:17 where we read, "As iron sharpens iron, so one man sharpens another." Relationships were meant to invigorate us and bring the wonderful aspect of friendship into our lives. Not all relationships will bring the same depth and enjoyment into our lives, nor are they meant to do so. The grocery boy who is bagging our groceries will not bring the same level of friendship to us as a dear friend that will allow us to share very vulnerable information without rejecting us. However, the grocery boy can add a spark to our day if he is friendly and respectful, and we have the privilege of adding a spark to his day when we treat him with respect.

H. Norman Wright provides a helpful guide to building positive relationships in his book, <u>HOW TO GET ALONG WITH ALMOST ANYONE</u>. Wright emphasizes that "Before you can lovingly get along with others as Christ commanded, you must learn to accept and love yourself." P.26 We agree with this statement wholeheartedly; which is why part I on building self-esteem, precedes the section on relationships.

Wright also agrees that not all relationships have the same degree of importance in our lives. Some relationships are minimal, surface-level relationships; other relationships might be moderate, strong, or quality relationships. In minimal relationships no emotional support is given or received; this changes as we move into stronger relationships, with the most effort being put into building and maintaining the quality relationships. This would include marital relationships and to a somewhat lesser degree, people belonging to a close network of friends. This might be a cell group that meets to study the

Bible and build community with one another. If we feel safe to reveal our inner struggles in this group, then the relationships in this group have become quality relationships.

Let's examine some components of building healthy relationships.

PRIORITIZE RELATIONSHIPS:

The first thing we need to do is to prioritize time to spend with our spouse, family and friends to build strong relationships. Healthy relationships do not happen automatically just because we are related to someone. This is very evident when we look at what happens with siblings from the same family who live many miles apart. Often, we feel closer to friends who live nearby, than we do to siblings who live in another city, province, or country. But even close proximity is not enough; we still have to schedule time to get together and build those relationships.

Assertive people feel confident, having a healthy self-esteem, and enjoy social activities where they have the opportunity to meet new people. They will often take the initiative to organize a social gathering, and have a wonderful time interacting with many different people.

In our office we encounter people who prioritize their jobs or careers over nurturing their relationships. This is very damaging to married couples or other close relationships. Sometimes single people expect a romantic relationship to blossom without any effort on their part. It is important to step out of our comfort zone and join clubs or church groups where we can meet other people with like interests.

* * *

Monica was hesitant to meet many new people at first, but when she started feeling better about herself, she found she really enjoyed getting together with the new friends she had made, both at Youth Centre and at the church she was attending. It seemed each week she met someone new and she rejoiced at how her circle of friends had enlarged. Soon, she took the courageous step of inviting a few friends to her basement suite for a simple meal after church.

When she had lived at home, Monica had some friends at school, but she had never invited them to her home; she would not want them to meet her parents who might be hung over. Nor would she want them to see their unkempt house.

* * *

Louise was a real home-body; she found it very intimidating to attend any of Tom's office parties so she usually begged off, pretending to be sick. When she couldn't get out of going, she stayed on the periphery, hoping no one would notice. Mostly, she felt she needed to stay at home in case Tom would call, so she didn't have many close friends at all.

* * *

Jack was nervous about meeting new people; he was worried about making a good impression, and since this put a lot of pressure on him, he avoided social events unless they were scheduled by his office. At times, he would also attend other social events, provided they would afford him the opportunity to showcase himself.

* * *

Samantha was a carefree teenager and had lots of friends, but her circle of close friends changed constantly. She often acted deviously, lying to some friends to avoid including them in an activity she would do with a different group of friends.

* * *

Chapter II

ASSERTIVE COMMUNICATION SKILLS

Kathy's morning had gone by very quickly; feeding three children and getting the two oldest ones out the door to school was always a juggling act in the mornings. Her husband Bob, had left for the office before the children awoke since he had an early morning board meeting. When the two older children were finally on their way to school, Kathy removed the baby's bib, wiped her face and hands, and set her down so she could toddle off to play with the building blocks in the family room.

After loading the dishwasher and sweeping up the crumbs that had fallen on the kitchen floor, most of the morning was gone. Kathy took a peak into the family room and saw that the baby was contentedly playing with her toys. The older children would be eating their lunches at school and she wasn't expecting Bob home for lunch so she decided she would take down the Christmas tree that was still standing in the living room.

Kathy picked up ten month old Cari under one arm while she gathered a few favorite toys with her other hand, and carried them into the living room. She got the baby settled in a safe area, then hauled out the decoration boxes and started to take the ornaments down. As she did so, she recalled the joy of seeing

Cari clap her hands with delight when she saw the Christmas tree for the first time.

Just as Kathy reached up for the star at the top of the tree, she heard the key in the door. Bob opened the door and walked in, stopping to pick up the baby and swing her in the air till she squealed. He set her down again and went to give Kathy a hug. As he did so, he said, "Why are you doing this now? If you'd leave it until tonight, I could help you."

"Why are you telling me what to do?" demanded Kathy, squirming out of his embrace.

"Honey, I'm not telling you what to do, it's just that this is a big job and I'd like to help you but I need to go back to the office in half an hour."

"I didn't ask you to help and I'm doing just fine. I didn't expect you home for lunch so I'm afraid you'll have to help yourself!"

Bob made himself a sandwich and decided to eat it on his way back to the office. He was sad as he drove away from home. Kathy always seemed to misinterpret what he was saying lately. He knew they needed to learn to communicate better but would Kathy be willing to go for help with him? She seemed so defensive.

* * *

After scheduling time for relationships, the next thing we need to do is practice good communication skills. In our office we ask couples to complete a questionnaire which helps us to evaluate the major areas that require improvement in their relationship. Without question, the area in which most couples have the lowest score is the area of communication.

TAKE TIME TO COMMUNICATE:

It seems that while we are dating we can spend hours talking to one another on the phone or over a cold drink or a romantic dinner. After the wedding ceremony many couples talk to each other less and less; some couples indicate that they are afraid to tell their spouse how they feel, or to ask for what they really want.

When we counsel couples in a pre-marital session, it seems strange to suggest that they need to schedule time to talk; however, it is important to do this. Instead of taking each other for granted now that we are married, we need to show continuing interest in each other by talking every day. We need to take time to discuss our goals and dreams as well as being vulnerable enough to share our fears and regrets. Some days we won't have overly important things to discuss but even then, we need to show an interest in each other by asking about their day.

If we are having some problems, we need to take time to talk about them and try to resolve them before they intensify. However, many couples clam up and focus on the faults they see in their spouse while feeling sorry for themselves. This is the typical passive response. Couples who blame each other by being verbally or physically abusive are using the aggressive response. And the worst response is the passive/aggressive response where couples speak to each other sarcastically or give each other the silent treatment.

Let's examine healthy, assertive communication skills that will help us build healthy relationships.

MARTHA FEHR, M.A. *with* WES FEHR, PH.D.

NECESSARY COMPONENTS FOR EFFECTIVE COMMUNICATION:

There are three main components necessary for effective communication to take place: a **message** sent, a **message received**, and the **message understood**. After people take **time** to communicate with one another, next it is important that we send messages correctly, that we make an effort to receive the messages sent, and make sure that we understand the message correctly.

SENDING THE MESSAGE:

The person who is talking is sending a message. It is important that we talk to our spouse and to our friends, but one of the dangers we face in talking is that sometimes we want to do all the talking and we don't give the other person equal opportunity to state their point of view. When we are counseling a married couple where one person wants to do all the talking, we suggest they use an egg timer, set it for a few minutes only and stop talking when the egg timer runs out, set it for the same time and allow the other person to respond. The new person talking needs to abide by the same rule when they are speaking. We even use this egg timer right in the counseling office when both people in the room are trying to out-talk each other.

RESPECTFUL WORDS:

When we remind ourselves that the main ingredient in assertiveness is respect, it follows that this respect should also be evident in how we speak to each other. This is a reasonable assumption, yet how many times do we actually speak with disrespect. This seems to happen especially with our own family, our spouse, our children, and sometimes our extended families.

While we are dating, we use the utmost respect in how we speak to our date; after being married for some time, we take each other for granted more and more, and as a result we often speak angry, disrespectful words to one another. A client choked back sobs as she described how her husband berated her as a useless b_____ who can never do anything right, and who has ruined his whole life! He used many other very derogatory words to describe her.

Another client made a good point when she responded assertively to her husband when he spoke with a rude tone of voice while complaining about something she had not done. She looked at her husband and quietly asked, "Would you speak to your banker the way you just spoke to me?" He couldn't answer her since he knew he wouldn't speak disrespectfully to his banker and he knew it had been wrong for him to speak so disrespectfully to his wife.

Speaking with disrespect will seriously damage relationships. Many of us as children repeated the little verse, "Sticks and stones will break my bones, but words will never hurt me!" As adults we've realized that just the opposite is true. When our physical bodies are injured they are able to heal much more quickly than our emotions. When someone speaks rude, degrading words to us it is very hard to heal because our self-esteem takes a hit. Even when we have a fairly healthy self-esteem, we tend to second guess ourselves when we hear those disrespectful words, especially if this happens repeatedly. Again the Golden Rule holds true in how we speak; we could say, "Speak unto others in the same way that you would want others to speak to you."

I need to make a special point about the fact that as parents, we need to speak respectfully to our children at every age. Sometimes we realize the importance of speaking respectfully to other adults, but we carelessly speak disrespectfully to our children. We are sinning against our children if we treat them with disrespect. Secondly, we are powerful role models for our children so it is important to present positive role models. We cannot expect our children to speak to us respectfully if we do not speak respectfully to them. We will also find that the reward of speaking with respect to our children will result in more obedient, happy children.

OPENNESS AND HONESTY:

Communication between husband and wife should be open, honest, and vulnerable. In other relationships the degree of openness will depend on the depth of the relationship. We all have baggage that we bring with us into new relationships; we would not be wise to be very open about our baggage when we first meet someone new. As we learn to know each other better, we will begin to share more of ourselves with one another. Eventually, we may feel safe to share our baggage if we have learned that the other person can be trusted with it.

It's not only romantic relationships that form deep bonds; sometimes relationships between two women or two men go very deep. In I Samuel 18-20, we read about the deep relationship of David and Jonathan who both spoke openly of their love for each other. David and Jonathan had such a deep, loving relationship that they could be open and honest with each other about everything. David even shared with Jonathan the fact that he feared Jonathan's father, King Saul, wanted to kill him. Jonathan desperately hoped this wasn't true, but he listened to David, checked it out, and helped him escape when he found out that David was right.

Part of being open and honest in our communication involves being able to express our feelings with close friends, without feeling shame. Jesus modeled this for us when His good friend Lazarus died. Even though Jesus knew that He would raise Lazarus from the dead, when He went to the home of Mary and Martha and saw Mary weeping, "He groaned in spirit and was troubled." John 11:33NKJV and in v. 35 we read that "Jesus wept."

Proverbs 25:11 says, "A word fitly spoken is like apples of gold in settings of silver." The words we say to one another are powerful; they have the power to encourage or discourage. Hebrews 3:13 says, "But encourage one another daily...so that none of you may be hardened by sin's deceitfulness." To maintain healthy relationships, we need to make sure that our words will encourage, rather than discourage. It is important to give credit for effort, not only for success.

In his book, <u>Bringing Up Kids Without Tearing Them Down</u>, Dr. Kevin Leman quotes Rudolf Dreikurs, "Encouragement is more important than any other aspect of child raising. It is so important that the lack of it can be considered the basic cause for misbehaviour. A misbehaving child is a discouraged child. Each child needs continuous encouragement as a plant needs water. He cannot grow and develop and gain a sense of belonging without encouragement."p.163

Dr. Leman goes on to caution that praise is not the same as encouragement. "Praise says 'You're great because you did something.' Encouragement says 'It's great that something was done and I appreciate it.'" P.181. In other words, praise is tied to the other person's value while encouragement acknowledges their strong effort.

Assertive people learn to know when they can share freely, and when it might be wise not to say too much.

* * *

Monica used to feel that she needed to apologize for her background and often gave out more information than was necessary. With time, she learned that it was okay to simply let people know that she had grown up in a dysfunctional home and to express gratitude to God for where she was now. If no one asked about her family, she didn't feel the need to say anything about them at all. Slowly Monica made a few very close friends and gradually she began to share more about her past, receiving encouragement from her friends, and often giving just as much encouragement to others.

One Sunday evening, Monica told her friends that a guy named Kevin had asked her out for coffee the night before. He was cute and she had seen him before at the youth centre, so she agreed to meet him. She told the girls that when their orders came, Kevin immediately launched into an account of his past which included a lot of bad choices and some weird things.

Monica knew that in the past she had shared too much, and now she asked her girlfriends what they thought about Kevin. She wondered why he would share so much when this was the first time they had actually met.

Monica's friends cautioned her not to get too involved with Kevin because sharing so much so soon was a big red flag for them. Monica was relieved that her feelings were confirmed, and she resolved to take things slow, if in fact, she would ever meet with him again.

* * *

Because Louise didn't have many close friends, she didn't have many opportunities to share deeply with anyone. Sometimes when Tom stayed at the office and worked late, she wished she had a friend with whom she could share her worries. When she did attend a social function, she talked only about very surface topics like the weather, unless she could hide and avoid conversation entirely.

* * *

Jack was inwardly nervous at social events but he put on a brave face and kept up a steady stream of engaging whoever was available, in a conversation about business activities. His low self-esteem led him to believe that it was important for him to prove to everyone who would listen, that he was a very intelligent, successful person.

By sticking to business topics, Jack avoided open and honest conversation during social events. Sadly, Jack was no different at home; his wife, Sue didn't know the real Jack – what did he really feel about their marriage? Did he feel trapped? Was he ashamed of her? Did he really feel as confident and assured as he appeared or did he have fears?

Sue didn't know the real Jack, but then, neither did Jack know the real Sue. Jack never seemed interested in her day so she didn't tell him much about her day, or about her deep longing for a more intimate relationship with him.

* * *

Samantha's conversations, being a typical teenager, were usually centered on which musical group was her favorite, what she wanted to buy next, and to which party she hoped to be invited.

There were times when Samantha wished she could talk to her mother about some of her fears and self-doubt, but her mother always seemed too busy or too tired. Samantha did have one friend at school that seemed to care when she was upset. A few times she shared what was bothering her, but most of the time,

Samantha had not learned to have open, honest and vulnerable communication with anyone.

HEARING THE MESSAGE OR LISTENING:

When we set out to build relationships with others, it can be tempting to tell the other person all about ourselves. Instead, we should demonstrate a desire to get to know them by asking them about themselves. H. Norman Wright says:

> Listening is an expression of love since it involves caring enough to take seriously what another person is communicating. When you listen lovingly, you invite that person into your life as a guest. When people know you hear them, they will trust you and feel safe with you. And if you are a good listener, others will be more apt to invite you into their lives as a guest. P.86

One way of demonstrating that we are interested in what others are saying, is by having good eye contact. This does not mean that we should stare into their eyes continually, but that we should not hesitate to look directly into their eyes from time to time.

Good body language is also important. We should lean towards them with a facial expression that says, "I want to hear what you have to say." Some people have a habit of looking past the person who is speaking or glancing around the room; this clearly demonstrates a lack of interest in what the person has to say. Walking away from someone who is talking to you is also body language that can be extremely hurtful to the person who is talking. This usually happens if the person talking is going on and on; this can be difficult for the listener, but instead of walking away, he should explain that he needs to leave.

When we are truly interested in what someone says to us it can be demonstrated by the fact that we will use a follow-up question, in the conversation, or even several days later. It could also be demonstrated by our actions. Many years ago, a friend and I were chatting and I laughingly told her that because I love chocolate so much, it's dangerous to open the bag of chocolate chips unless I make cookies with them right away. Once the bag is opened, it is tempting to sneak a few more chocolate chips every time I open the fridge door and sometimes the whole bag disappears before they even get into a cookie. Sometime later, my friend brought me a dozen cupcakes that were decorated with icing and lots of chocolate chips. This demonstrated to me that she was a true friend who had taken note of what I had said, and she blessed me with a delicious gift!

UNDERSTANDING THE MESSAGE OR REFLECTIVE COMMUNICATION:

Talking and listening are not enough for effective communication; understanding is a very important component. There are a number of reasons that misunderstandings occur when we try to communicate with someone. One reason could be that the two people who are having the conversation, come from different backgrounds. As a result, each may use certain words or phrases which may have different meanings for each of them.

Other times, the speaker is not talking clearly. The best way for understanding to occur is through the use of reflective communication. To do this, we need to repeat back to the speaker what they have just said, as we understood it. If we understood them correctly, the other person can simply acknowledge that we have heard them. If however, we misunderstood, they have an opportunity to correct our understanding immediately, and in a pleasant manner. At least fifty percent of any problem is resolved by using reflective communication for better understanding.

Reflective communication is sometimes called active listening or mirroring; all of these descriptive words used in connection with listening, help us to see that effort is needed on our part as we seek to truly hear what the other person has to say, as well as to understand their feelings around this issue.

Understanding is what is important; agreeing is not necessarily essential. If we find that we cannot agree with the other person's point of view, we need to allow for the fact that we all have the right to our own opinions. Rather than arguing the point, we might want to say something like, "Can we agree to disagree on this point? You have a right to your opinion and I have a right to mine."

Chapter III
RESOLVING CONFLICT ASSERTIVELY

Roseanne awoke slowly and realized she had been lying in one position for too long and her left hip which usually gave her trouble was beginning to throb. She knew it was time to turn over and give her hip a break. As she did so, she glanced over at the other side of the bed; it was empty! Where was Ian? He had come to bed only twenty minutes after she had gone to bed; they had chatted for a few minutes before she fell into a sound sleep.

Roseanne decided to get up to see if Ian was sick and needed her help. He was nowhere in the living room or the family room so she went down the stairs towards his den. As she came up behind him, he jumped and changed the screen on his computer. Roseanne hadn't seen much but she did know that what she had seen wasn't something that made her happy.

Ian demanded, "Why are you sneaking around and scaring the dickens out of me?!"

"I wasn't sneaking around," countered Roseanne, "And if you were in bed where you are supposed to be at 3:00 a.m., I wouldn't have come looking for you, to see if you were sick and needed my help! What are you doing down here?"

"I couldn't sleep, so I thought I'd come down and get a head start on the office files for tomorrow." replied Ian.

Roseanne raised her eyebrows and asked, "Was that scantily dressed woman part of your research for tomorrow?!"

"I wasn't looking at any scantily dressed woman; you need to get your eyes checked!"

"Ian," replied Roseanne, "I don't need my eyes checked, and yes, I did see a scantily dressed woman on your computer screen. I need my rest for work tomorrow, so I'm going to go back to bed; I don't want to talk about this tonight, but after work tomorrow, we need to have a serious talk. I hope you're not into porn because if you are, I need you to know that it would hurt me deeply. I love you so much and I try to meet your needs sexually. If that isn't enough for you, then we have some very serious issues."

Ian jumped up from his chair and brushed past Roseanne. "I'll be sleeping in the den tonight! How dare you accuse me of being into porn!"

Relationships do not always run smoothly and when conflicts arise it is important to resolve them as soon as possible. It is especially important to resolve relationships between husband and wife and with family members, including extended family. As I write this, it is only a few weeks before Christmas when most families plan get-togethers, regardless of whether they enjoy being together or not. Clients who are not assertive allow themselves to be manipulated into attending these family functions even though they know they will be tense throughout the gathering. It becomes an even bigger problem when the family members live in different cities and coming for the family function includes staying over for a day or even a week.

Almost every family has some issues which cause tension; we might also experience tension with co-workers or neighbors. The difference is that we may not always remain at the same job, or live in the same neighborhood, but we will always be related to our family. Therefore, it is important for us to know how to resolve conflicts. The skills we use for resolving relationship problems in our family can also be used for those difficult co-workers or neighbors.

ADDRESS ISSUES:

We need to address issues; this is one of the most important skills in maintaining healthy relationships. Roseanne went back to bed and after tossing and turning for another hour, she finally fell asleep. In the morning Roseanne wondered if it had all been a bad dream; Ian was up and had made the coffee. He poured her a cup and asked if she would like a scrambled egg for breakfast. She loved how he doted on her in the mornings, knowing that mornings were not her favorite time of the day.

Roseanne didn't like conflict so she smiled, nodded, and sat down to enjoy her coffee. Looking at him now, bent over the stove, she knew why she loved him so much. Perhaps she had been seeing something totally innocent on the computer screen last night. Maybe she shouldn't say anything tonight, after all, why spoil the atmosphere?

Ephesians 4:15 NIV, encourages us to address issues by, "…speaking the truth in love,…" If we do so, we have a promise that "…we will in all things grow up into Him who is the Head, that is, Christ." In other words, the Bible indicates that it is a mature thing to address issues with others. Speaking the truth in love indicates that we are not to be aggressive, angrily accusing the offender about what they did. Neither should we be passive, allowing others to hurt us without any protest. Neither extreme would improve the relationship; the only healthy response is to speak the truth in a firm, but loving way. Addressing the issue in a loving way indicates that we care more about the relationship than the offense.

During the day at the office, Roseanne thought about the passage from Ephesians 4:15 and she decided that even though it might get unpleasant, she needed to address the issue with Ian. With greater resolve, she determined to bring up the topic after dinner. She reminded herself that she needed to give Ian an opportunity to explain what he had been doing on the computer last night and she needed to listen with an open mind. She actually hoped that Ian had a reasonable explanation.

At the same time, Roseanne knew that she needed to speak with confidence as she explained her feelings about what she had seen last night. She determined to use "I feel" sentences rather than using blaming sentences that start with "You…" She knew that she had been wise not to attempt to address the issue at three in the morning, but she was still feeling anxious.

Ian had been very defensive and aggressive in his reaction to her questions last night; she hoped he would be more amicable tonight. This was not to be! When the attempt at resolving the issue that evening failed, Ian and Roseanne booked an appointment with a counselor and with his guidance, they were able to see that Ian's experiment with pornography was only a symptom of deeper problems. It took several months of seeing the counselor and learning to be open and honest with each other as well as addressing issues assertively, before they felt confident they could handle any problem on their own.

Other Scriptures also affirm an assertive way of addressing issues; in Leviticus 19:17-18 NIV we read, "Do not hate your brother in your heart. Rebuke your neighbor frankly so you will not share in his guilt. Do not seek revenge or bear a grudge against one of your people, but love your neighbor as yourself. I am the Lord."

God knows that if our brother has offended us, we will react in one of two ways; either we will seek revenge or we will hold a grudge. In holding a grudge, we often review the offense over and over in our minds. Neither of these reactions is conducive to having a healthy relationship with the person who offended us; in fact, we will be sinning. Now both people in the relationship are guilty of sinning against God; the perpetrator of the offense because of what s/he did, and the victim of the offense who is now seeking revenge or holding a grudge. The only positive way of rescuing this relationship is to rebuke the offender frankly, in a way that he can retain his dignity while the victim can legitimately address his hurt.

My (Martha's) mother is 94 and living in an Assisted Living Complex where she reaches out to develop friendships with many of the other residents. I try to call my mother at least weekly, sometimes more often. Since mom is very hard of hearing, I am happy when she has many things to share with me about her daily experiences with the other residences; this means there will be less that I need to say, hoping that mom can hear me.

Mom is a very friendly, outgoing person who makes friends with people that are not readily accepted by others in the complex. About six months ago, a woman named Barbara came to live in the same complex, just a few doors down from my mother's room. Barbara had been living with her son and daughter-in-law and was most unhappy about her placement in the facility. She was not only angry at her son and daughter-in-law for placing her in this complex; she was frightened due to being unfamiliar with the building and with the rules that governed the residents. Mom realized how frightened and lonely Barbara was so she took her under her wing, waiting to walk with her to the dining room, showing her where she could find the laundry facilities, and visiting with her in her room.

During our weekly chats, mom often admitted that it was hard to spend time with Barbara due to her surly attitude, but she felt that she should be willing to do this because no one else reached out to her. Even her son and daughter-in-law visited very infrequently. Little by little, Barbara adjusted to her surroundings and didn't rely on mom quite so much. Mom enjoyed a little more freedom but she was still there for Barbara when she was needed.

Barbara is failing fairly quickly in her mental capacity and talk is that she will soon be moved to a facility where she will receive more care. Her weakness in this area showed itself with a very mean statement to my mother. Barbara tends to misplace some of her things and this particular day she told my mom, "You're in my room so often, and every time you come in, you steal one of my sweaters!" My mother was very upset, to say the least; she denied the accusation, then she went straight to the front desk where she reported what had happened. The girls at the front desk assured mom that "Barbara has problems; she will be moved to another facility where she will get more care as soon as space opens up. Please don't take this personally."

Mom could understand this but she knew that her relationship with Barbara had been damaged and she wanted to be able to be the friend that Barbara needed. A few weeks later, mom saw her opportunity. Only Barbara and mom were sitting in a little conversation area; no one was coming down the halls from either side, so mom decided this was the time to address the issue with Barbara. Mom wasn't sure if Barbara was in a head space that would allow her to understand what mom was saying, but she was determined to try and resolve this issue.

Mom reminded Barbara, "Do you remember the day that you accused me of stealing sweaters from your room?"

Barbara answered, "Yes".

Mom continued, "And do you know that I would never steal anything from you?" Again Barbara answered in the affirmative. This was going well so mom asked, "And can you say that you are sorry for accusing me of stealing your sweaters?"

Again, Barbara answered, "Yes."

Perhaps mom should have been able to accept that "Barbara has problems" and shouldn't have pushed for this apology but she knew that for her the relationship would be damaged until she addressed the issue. Upon hearing Barbara's agreement that she was sorry, mom walked up to her, held out her hand, and declared, "Now we're friends again, right?" Barbara returned her handshake and their friendship was back on track.

Mom heeded the Scripture from Leviticus 19:17-18. She did not want to have negative feelings toward Barbara; she also wanted to help Barbara change her ways of easily accusing others falsely.

Passive people who don't speak up for themselves are not obeying this Scripture; neither are aggressive people who angrily defend themselves. Passive/aggressive people may not speak up or become outwardly aggressive, but they may try to hurt others in sneaky, cowardly ways to pay others back for hurting them. These dysfunctional ways of dealing with conflict will lead to disintegration or total loss of the relationship.

The assertive person is able to "speak the truth in love" because they know this is the best way to preserve and enhance the relationship. They also have the courage to speak up because it is the way to respect themselves and the other person. It is disrespectful to walk away from the relationship, or to be abusive to the other person in any way.

Our son Randy faced a very difficult situation recently where he worked hard to return "good for evil" to his superior at work; after trying to cope with this for some time, Randy decided it was time to address this issue.

Randy is a pilot, a first officer at the time of this incident, whose captain was a very angry man. The captain prevented our son from gaining extra experience at the controls while on an important mission, and threatened to "punch him in the face" every few days. As a Christian, Randy continued to show respect to the captain, recognizing his authority over him.

In Matthew 5:39 we are encouraged to, "...turn the other cheek..." These words were first spoken to the Israelites who were under Roman rule and often a soldier would force someone to carry his baggage for some distance. Jesus encouraged the Israelite, "...whoever compels you to go one mile, go with him two." Randy was "turning the other cheek" as well as returning "good for evil" in that he not only continued to show respect, but he worked hard to load the plane, do the record keeping, and check the weather forecast. Randy had also complimented the captain on his expertise in the cockpit. Meanwhile, the captain continued to be surly and he let Randy know that he has indeed, popped other people in the face.

One day the captain screamed uncontrollably at Randy while he was refueling the plane. When they were finished, Randy spoke quietly, but firmly, to his captain, "Shawn, you know that

I respect your ability as a professional pilot. However, do you feel your treatment of me is professional?"

Shawn replied, "I'm treating you exactly as you deserve to be treated!"

"Really?" said Randy, "You think threatening me, cursing me and losing it all the time is professional?!"

"Take it up with the boss if you're not happy," was Shawn's response.

Randy replied, "It is my practice to always go to the individual before going over his or her head." The captain walked away without a response but it seemed that he actually treated Randy with a little more respect for the rest of the day. This is often the result of being assertive.

The Bible teaches us the wisdom of addressing issues. In Matthew 5:23-24 as well as in Matthew 18:15-17 we are instructed how to respond when someone has sinned against us. This sin could be something relatively simple like speaking to us disrespectfully, or something more serious. In any case, the Bible does not encourage us to keep quiet and simply let others treat us poorly. In Matthew 5:23 & 24 it says, "Therefore, if you are offering your gift at the altar and there remember that your brother has something against you, leave your gift there in front of the altar. First go and be reconciled to your brother; then come and offer your gift."

The passage in Matthew 18 gives us more specific instructions on how to be reconciled to the brother that hurt us. It reads, "If your brother sins against you, go and show him his fault, just between the two of you. If he listens to you, you have won your brother over. But if he will not listen, take one or two along, so that every matter may be established by the testimony of two or three witnesses. If he refuses to listen to them, tell it to the church; and if he refuses to listen even to the church, treat him as you would a pagan or a tax collector." This is serious business. God knows that if we do not address issues, it will do nothing for that relationship.

In fact, Proverbs 28:23 tells us that, "He who rebukes a man will in the end gain more favor, than he who has a flattering tongue."

An author I was reading recently believes that the reference to slapping someone on the cheek in Matthew 5:39 has to do with showing contempt. Certainly Randy's captain had shown contempt for him while Randy continued to "turn the other cheek". If the captain should ever dare to actually hit Randy, this is where Randy would draw the line; he would defend himself.

Keeping quiet about hurts inflicted by others will often result in resentment and bitterness. This is not what God wants for us. Hebrews 12:15 says, "See to it that no one comes short of the grace of God; that no root of bitterness springing up causes trouble, ..." Proverbs 27:5,6 says, "Better is open rebuke than hidden love. Wounds from a friend can be trusted, but an enemy multiplies kisses." A true friend will rebuke us when we have hurt them while a passive/aggressive person may flatter us rather than rebuke us in love.

While watching a rerun of <u>Touched by an Angel</u> I saw a perfect illustration of the damage that can happen to a relationship when we do not address issues. In the storyline, two middle-aged people, let's call them Tom and Lorie, were very upset with each other and they needed help from the angels to deal with the conflict between them. They lived next door to each other and they used every opportunity to make life miserable for each other; as a result, they were both miserable.

Apparently, when these two were kids, they used to climb up in the tree between the two properties, and enjoyed each other's company as best friends. This friendship grew, and when they were sixteen, Tom gave Lorie a rose, placed in a box that usually holds a ring, and asked her to marry him. When she said, "Yes!" he promised to buy her a ring some day.

Lorie excitedly asked a neighbor to sew her wedding dress but she never got to use it; Tom's father didn't allow the wedding to take place. He told Tom it would be utter nonsense to throw his life away by marrying Lorie at this time. Tom was sent away to a school far away and the two young lovers didn't speak to each other for several years.

Years later Tom came back to the town to become the pastor of the local church and Lorie came back as the town's doctor; they moved back into their family homes, next door to each other. Living next door to each other, the couple continued to feed their anger for one another; that is, until Tom's grandson, Robert, came to spend a week with him.

At first, Lorie tried to use Robert against Tom, but when Robert was seriously injured in a traffic accident, Tom and Lorie put their differences aside long enough to look after Robert's needs. As a result, they also engaged in some serious discussions. They discovered that Tom had written to Lorie many times, telling her of his continuing love for her. When he had not received any replies from her, he assumed she was angry at him and he gave up on the relationship, but harbored bitterness against Lorie, a bitterness that had grown stronger with the passing years.

Lorie, on the other hand, had hoped and waited eagerly for a letter from Tom, but when none ever came, she assumed he no longer loved her and she gave up on the relationship; she too, harbored bitterness against Tom.

Since Tom's father had been the mailman in those days, they realized now that he must have intercepted all of Tom's letters which explained why Lorie had never received even one. If Tom and Lorie had addressed this issue years ago, they would have saved themselves a lot of anger, bitterness and lost years. As it was, they ended up getting married before the end of the show, determined to make the best of the years they had left. This is fiction but the same scenario has been played out in real life, many times over, although not necessarily with the positive conclusion.

With regards to addressing issues, we need to think before we speak; in fact, we need to decide if the issue that is bothering us is important enough to address. We should always remember to major on the major issues and let some of the minor issues go. Being courageous enough to address issues doesn't mean that we should confront others about every little issue.

When we confront someone we also need to be careful not to assign a motive to their actions, or assassinate their character. We need to discuss the action itself, and give the other person a chance to explain why they did, what they did. If their explanations are reasonable, we need to accept that they were not trying to be hurtful. If however, their actions were inexcusable, we need to tell them what the consequences will be if they do not change their unacceptable behavior.

There will be times when someone else will confront us about something. At those times, it will be important for us not to be defensive. A mature, assertive person will be willing to listen to what the other person has to say. We need to look at someone's rebuke as a challenge pointing out where we need to grow and learn to do things better. The temptation will be to feel like we don't measure up, but an assertive mindset will help us to see that this is really an opportunity to continue growing as a healthy person.

God is our example in addressing issues. In Genesis 3, we read about the first sin by Adam and Eve when they ate from the tree of good and evil. When God came to walk with them in the garden, Adam and Eve hid. The open relationship they had had with God before they had sinned was disrupted. God could have left them alone and waited for them to come to Him and apologize. But God did not do this; instead, He pursued the relationship with Adam and Eve. God came to them and addressed the issue. A little later, we will look at how God addressed the issue of their disobedience.

We should learn from God and address issues rather than allow a relationship to end. We should not allow pride or fear to keep us from addressing issues.

* * *

Monica listened carefully to the lesson and realized she could learn from this. She had been wondering what to do about Mrs. Peabody, a little, white-haired lady who also attended the church. She was sweet, but she could be a little over-bearing. Whenever Mrs. Peabody saw Monica, she would rush over and greet her like a long-lost relative, almost crushing her with a vice-like hug. Now Monica realized that she needed to talk to Mrs. Peabody instead of trying to avoid her as she had often done. She had her chance the very next Sunday. She saw Mrs. Peabody as she was leaving the church after the service. She went over and gave her a gentle hug and said, "I need to talk to you. I appreciate you and your friendliness. However, I want you to know that I would like you to hug me a little less hard. If

I'm afraid you'll get me in a vice-like hold, I will try to avoid you and I don't want to do that to you. Could you do that for me?"

Mrs. Peabody apologized and agreed to hug her gently, at which Monica gave her another hug, and the two parted happily.

* * *

Louise was so afraid of conflict that she did not address issues. If she sensed that Tom was upset, she tried to avoid being alone with him. If Tom was angry and yelled at her for something, she was quick to take responsibility and apologize.

One time Tom was hurrying out of the room and he bumped into the side table, knocking their expensive, decorator lamp to the floor. Louise jumped as the lamp made a loud crashing noise, and immediately cried out, "I'm sorry! I'm so sorry!" Tom looked at her with disgust; walked out the door and slammed the door behind him. Tom knew that he was responsible for breaking the lamp, but if Louise wanted to accept blame, he would let her.

* * *

Jack addressed issues easily, but he did so in an aggressive manner. When he reviewed the work of the other accountants he was quick to point out trivial mistakes, and he did so in a degrading way. He did not hesitate to berate another accountant in front of co-workers, leaving the accountant feeling shamed and helpless. Everyone knew they dared not say anything in their own defense or he would be even more biting in his reply.

Jack was also quick to find fault with his wife about almost everything; from how she took care of their son to how she cooked or did the laundry. When she had tried to speak up for herself in the past she had been severely reprimanded; now she simply accepted his verbal abuse and tried not to annoy him.

* * *

Samantha addressed issues by using a whining, immature tone of voice with her mother. She often felt that her mother was being over-protective with her in some ways, but because she did not know how to address this issue in a mature, assertive way, her mother brushed her concerns aside.

Samantha also tried to put her mother on a guilt trip; this worked quite well, since her mother already felt guilty about having divorced her father. In this way, Samantha was able to get some things she wanted, yet she longed to have more meaningful conversations with her mother. Typical of teenagers, Samantha gossiped about her mother to her friends. It seemed to her that everyone was doing it, so to fit in, Samantha did it as well. Every so often, Samantha brought home a school friend who was thoroughly surprised to find Samantha's mother to be such a pleasant woman.

ASKING QUESTIONS:

Asking questions can be a wonderful tool to deepen friendships; however, we can also use questions in negative ways which could result in people avoiding a relationship with us. H. Norman Wright says that, "Some people use questions to deepen and enrich their relationships. But many people use questions as a weapon to pry, maneuver, gain advantage, attack, trap, set up, or break down the defenses of others." He also makes the point that some people use questions as barriers to keep others from getting too close to them. As long as they keep the other person talking about themselves, they won't have to reveal anything personal.

Even though questions can be used for negative reasons, the benefits of asking questions outweigh the negative. Questions are a good way of getting to know others and showing our interest in them. Questions can help us to understand the other person, especially when they behave in ways that are hurtful. Instead of nursing our hurt, we need to ask questions to try to understand what may have led to their inappropriate behavior; being willing to listen and really hear others is a godly thing to do. God is always ready to hear us and we need to do the same for each other. "He who answers before listening – that is his folly and his shame.", so reads Proverbs 18:13.

TO RESOLVE ISSUES:

That takes us back to the topic of addressing issues with others. First of all, we must remember to be respectful. It takes a lot of courage to ask someone to meet with us so that we can address a heavy topic. The people we need to confront might come to the meeting in a defensive mode, ready to attack us. How will we address the issue without further alienating them or increasing their defensiveness? When we have determined to ask questions for better understanding, it gives us the courage to address issues with someone who has hurt us because we can focus on what we want instead of giving in to fear of their reaction which keeps us silent.

Dr. David Burns devotes an entire chapter in his book to dealing with difficult people. He encourages us to use the techniques of inquiry, empathy, disarming, and negotiating. Inquiry refers to the request for information; in other words, the inquiry technique simply refers to asking questions for clarification. Empathy means "identifying with" or "understanding the feelings of another person." The disarming technique refers to taking away "any means of attack or defense" from the other person. And finally, to negotiate is to "confer with another person to reach an agreement." P.420-441

Let's look at a real life example of how using these techniques would work. In this example, Julie feels that Mary was avoiding her during a social event put on at her work place. Since Julie and Mary had been good friends for a long time, Julie felt hurt by this apparent snubbing. When Julie went home that night, she had trouble falling asleep because she couldn't help but wonder what had brought on this unusual behavior on Mary's part. Julie prayed about the situation and felt strongly that she needed to address the issue with Mary; she couldn't allow such a special relationship to disintegrate for no apparent reason. Once she had made a plan to talk to Mary, sleep came quickly.

The next morning Julie went straight to Mary's desk and suggested they meet for lunch at a nearby restaurant. When Mary hesitated, Julie told her, "I really need to talk to you. Do you think you could make it today?" Mary agreed and the two walked over to the restaurant as soon as their lunch break started. Julie waited until they had both ordered, then she addressed the issue without delay.

"Mary, I wanted to talk to you because we've been friends for a very long while and I never want anything to come between us. That's why I wanted to talk to you and find out if I have done something to hurt you; I felt like you avoided me all evening at the social. Is something wrong?"

Mary replied, "I didn't know it was that obvious, but yes, I was upset. I felt like you didn't want to be my friend anymore; I was hurt and I wanted to hurt you back!"

"Please give me more information Mary." replied Julie, "What made you think I didn't want to be your friend anymore; I don't understand." (Inquiry technique) Asking for more information lets the other person know that you are open to hearing and understanding them.

"You are spending so much time with the new girl Rhonda and the two of you are always laughing and looking like you're having so much fun, I really feel left out of your life. You haven't spent time with me for weeks!"

Julie replied, "I can see that you feel really hurt. I know that I would also feel hurt if I felt you didn't want my friendship any longer." (Empathy technique) "I'm beginning to understand that from your perspective, it felt like I was ignoring you." (Disarming technique) "But now that I've heard how you feel, can I explain what was really going on?" (Negotiating technique) "Rhonda is new and she needs a lot of help learning to use our computer programs; her former company used very different ones. The reason we laughed so much was because Rhonda kept making silly mistakes which had us both howling. She's a nice person and I want to be available to help her, but you will always be a very special friend. And by the way, it hasn't been weeks since we spent time together. Remember when we went for a quick coke after work last Tuesday?"

Mary reached over to squeeze Julie's hand, "You're right of course, Julie. Thanks for suggesting lunch today."

This was a very easy situation to resolve but the same techniques work when the issues are more heated. We can also employ these techniques when we are approached by someone who is upset with us and may criticize us harshly. God Himself, and Jesus, are our best examples of asking questions in difficult situations. Earlier we pointed out how God pursued His relationship with Adam and Eve by addressing the issue of their sin. Now we will see how God used the skill of asking questions in addressing the issue.

ASK INSTEAD OF ACCUSE TO PRESERVE DIGNITY:

When God came to walk in the garden with Adam and Eve, He asked the question, "Where are you?" because they had hidden themselves. Surely God, being God, knew where they had hidden themselves, so why would He ask the question? By asking the question, God was allowing them to take responsibility and preserve their dignity by coming forward to make amends and to preserve the relationship.

Asking questions gives the other person a chance to think before they answer rather than just making a defensive statement.

Adam and Eve did not admit their sin however; instead, they excused their hiding by saying, "I was afraid, because I was naked; and I hid myself." Again God asked, "Who told you that you were naked?" Genesis 3:10,11

Once more, God is giving Adam and Eve the opportunity to confess what they had done. When they did not do so, God came right to the core of the problem by asking, "Have you eaten from the tree of Life?"

Adam and Eve were still reluctant to confess their sin and when God asked this direct question, they started to blame shift. Adam blamed Eve, and even suggested God might be to blame because He had given Eve to him, and Eve blamed the serpent.

I wonder what would have happened if Adam had come forward and said, "God, I have sinned against You and I did not stand up for what I knew was right."

In spite of Adam and Eve's refusal to take responsibility, God did not address the blame shifting or the lying, but gave them further opportunity to come clean by asking, "What have you done?'

God continues to ask questions because He wants to give all of us the opportunity to take responsibility for our actions, and to restore our relationship with Him. We could do the same by asking a simple question like, "How did you feel about what happened?" to give the other person a chance to take responsibility for their fault in the situation.

TO DEFUSE ANGER:

God used questions with Cain as recorded in Genesis 4 where we read that Cain was very angry because his brother's offering was accepted, and his was not. God saw that he was angry and asked three questions, trying to engage Cain in talking about his anger in an effort to help him do things differently which would resolve his anger.

God asked, "Why are you angry? Why is your face downcast? If you do what is right, will you not be accepted?' Genesis 4:6-7

Cain however, did not listen. Instead, he was so angry that he killed his brother, Abel.

Again God came to him to ask, "Where is your brother?" Cain did not take responsibility but became defensive and arrogant. God did not allow His own emotions to be affected; instead, He simply asked again, "What have you done?" We too, need to keep our own anger under control, and by asking questions, help the other person to calm down when s/he sees that we are interested in hearing what they have to say.

TO FOSTER ACCEPTANCE VERSUS JUDGMENT:

Another time that we can use questions is when we feel judged or we see someone else judging a helpless person. Once, when

Jesus was teaching about the pitfalls of judging others, he told them, "Do not judge, or you too will be judged. For in the same way you judge others, you will be judged,..." Then He went on to ask, "Why do you look at the speck of sawdust in your brother's eye and pay no attention to the plank in your own eye? How can you say to your brother, 'Let me take the speck out of your eye,' when all the time there is a plank in your own eye?" Matthew 7:1-4. When someone else is judging us, we may be able to resolve the issue by asking them what they would do in a similar situation.

SANDWICH FORMULA:

The Sandwich Formula is another tool that will help us strengthen our relationships. It combines the skill of asking questions with the opportunity to encourage the people in our circle of friendship. In an earlier section of the book we talked about the importance of encouraging others. Hebrews 3:13 admonishes us to "...encourage each other daily..."; this is not a suggestion, it is a command. When we use the Sandwich Formula, we are drawing twice the attention to the positive as the negative. Furthermore, in addressing the negative, we use questions rather than accusations.

In the New Testament book of Philemon, we read the letter that Paul sent to a man named Philemon on behalf of a new believer, Onesimus. Onesimus had been Philemon's slave but he ran away and met Paul who introduced him to Jesus. Now Paul is asking Philemon to take Onesimus back, not only as a slave, but as a fellow believer.

> I always thank God when I pray for you, Philemon, because I keep hearing of your trust in the Lord Jesus, and your love for all of God's people. You are generous because of your faith. And I am praying that you will

really put your generosity to work, for in so doing you will come to an understanding of all the good things we can do for Christ. I myself have gained much joy and comfort from your love, my brother, because your kindness has so often refreshed the hearts of God's people.

That is why I am boldly asking a favor of you. I could demand it in the name of Christ because it is the right thing for you to do, but because of our love, I prefer just to ask you. So take this as a request from your friend Paul, an old man, now in prison for the sake of Jesus Christ. …

Yes, dear brother, please do me this favor for the Lord's sake. Give me this encouragement in Christ. I am confident as I write this letter that you will do what I ask and even more! Philemon 4-9;20

This letter is a model for us about how to use the "sandwich formula" when you need to bring up difficult topics with someone. Notice how Paul starts his letter to Philemon, the first slice of bread, by encouraging him for his trust in the Lord and his generosity. Then Paul moves on to the filling part of the sandwich in which he asks Philemon for a favor. Paul states that he could demand that Philemon do the right thing, but because of their friendship, he is asking Philemon to do this favor. Then in part three, the second slice of bread, Paul ends his letter by stating his confidence that Philemon will do the right thing.

This Sandwich Formula is also seen in the book of Revelation where Jesus sends messages to the churches of the day through John. In most cases the churches are commended for the good things they are doing in the first part of the address followed by a middle section which usually begins with "However" or "But". This section notes areas that displease God, where change needs to happen; usually the letter to the church ends on a positive note once again. An example of this is chapter two, verses two to six:

> I know what you do, how you work hard and never give up. I know you do not put up with the false teachings of evil people. You have tested those who say they are apostles but really are not, and you found they are liars. You have patience and have suffered troubles for my name and have not given up.

> But I have this against you: You have left the love you had in the beginning. So remember where you were before you fell. Change your hearts and do what you did at first. If you do not change, I will come to you and take away your lampstand from its place.

> But there is something you do that is right: you hate what the Nicolaitans do, as much as I.

METHOD OF DELIVERY:

In the Living translation of the Bible, Proverbs 16:21 reads as follows: "The wise are known for their understanding, and instruction is appreciated if it's well presented." It is so important to realize that often it is not <u>what</u> we say, as much as <u>how</u> we say something that ends up being offensive to the other person. Again, the skill of asking questions comes into play. As a parent, I believe our children would respond in a better way if we would say something like, "Could I ask you to do the dishes as soon as we finish eating since we want the house to be tidy when our friends drop in?" rather than saying, "You need to do the dishes as soon as we're finished eating; no dilly-dallying!".

The method of delivery is certainly important when we need to confront someone about their bad behavior. If we use an aggressive method of attacking the other person, they will be much more defensive than if we use the assertive approach. When we attack someone we are robbing them of their dignity which will damage the relationship. Why would they want to continue a relationship with us when we have just insulted them?

Using the Sandwich Formula is one way we can make sure we are using an appropriate method of delivery. When we make sure to affirm the good we see in someone, they feel valued as individuals and are able to hear the concern we have.

DISCUSS THE BEHAVIOR, NOT THE MOTIVE AND DON'T USE CHARACTER ASSASSINATION:

When we confront someone about a behavior, we need to stick to talking about the behavior; we should not assume that we know <u>why</u> they behaved the way they did. We need to be willing to listen to their explanation behind the behavior.

It is also imperative that we do not make sweeping, negative statements about their character; this person did something which made you unhappy but it doesn't mean their whole character is flawed.

RESPONDING VERSUS REACTING:

We used the word "respond" earlier; this is a very important word because when we respond we are being assertive. When we "react" it usually means we are being defensive in an aggressive or passive/aggressive manner. I like to come up with acrostics which help us to remember the most important aspects of a word. Look at the difference in whether we "react" or "respond" when we face a relationship conflict.

R – React without thinking	R – Respond after careful Thought
E – Extreme Emotions	E – Experience Satisfaction
A – Avoid Conflict	S – Seek Understanding
C – Closed Communications	P – Plan Goals for the Relationship
T – Try to Blame Others	O – Open, Honest Communication
	N – Negotiate Resolutions
	D – Delay Action

Reacting is what we do when we act without thinking about what we are doing. To respond to someone means that we are thinking about what we need to say or do, in response to what the other person has said or done. Reacting might mean that we are falling back into old habits and patterns of behaving.

RELATIONSHIPS ARE WORTH IT:

Conflict resolution is difficult but if the relationship is one that is important, it deserves the effort that it takes to resolve the conflict.

An example of a friendship which demonstrates many positive components is a friendship between Dr. Larry Crab and Dan Allender. In his foreword to Dan Allender's book, <u>The Wounded Heart,</u> Dr. Larry Crab says of their friendship, "Dan and I are knit together by a mutual loyalty, affection, and respect, developed through hard times and good that defines the word *friendship."* P.11. Here we have three important components of friendships: Mutual loyalty, Affection, and Respect.

Respect is the main ingredient in assertive speech and behavior and should be a part of every relationship. Mutual loyalty in a relationship means we will be willing to do the hard work of conflict resolution and the affection we feel for each other will only increase when we have come through some difficult times which included problem solving.

Chapter IV
FORGIVENESS AND ASSERTIVENESS

When a grieving mother stood in an Edmonton courtroom last month and publicly forgave the drunk driver who had killed her daughter, her actions seemed out of place in a society inundated with images of vigilante style justice.

Thus began the article in the Calgary Herald some years ago under the heading of "The Power of Forgive, Making the choice to forgive is the first step on the road to emotional, spiritual and physical recovery." The article continued,

Having to come face-to-face with someone who killed a loved one – let alone offer them words of forgiveness – is unthinkable.

However, Sandra Foot refused to subscribe to this way of thinking. On the sunny summer day that she offered her words of forgiveness, she also had to remember the fateful night of Oct. 1, 1997, when the accused crashed head-on into 18-year-old Kirsty Foot's car while driving her minivan the wrong way down Highway 16A near Edmonton.

During the trial, it was revealed that the accused was depressed over her failing marriage and had been drinking heavily.

An expert in human interactions says Foot's decision to forgive her daughter's killer could be the kindest thing she's ever done – for all those involved, but especially for herself. Michael McCullough, co-author of the book To Forgive is Human, says forgiving those who have harmed us is not only good for our hearts and minds: it's good for us physically.

The article says that McCullough has support in the medical community,

> To naturopath Dr. Bruce Lofting it makes sense that the act of forgiving can have a powerful effect on health. People respond to stress with a "fight or flight" response that drains the adrenal system, affecting their immune response and playing havoc with their metabolism.
>
> "Forgiveness is the ultimate in achieving a relaxation response," he says, "Like tears in crying, there is tremendous relief in completely forgiving."

* * *

In the previous chapter we discussed the importance of addressing issues using questions; now we need to talk about the next step which is that we need to make a choice to forgive the person who has offended us. Forgiveness is a very big part of being assertive.

Not all of us will have to face someone who has killed a loved one, but all of us will undoubtedly face the need to forgive a person who has harmed us in some way. As the newspaper article says, forgiveness benefits us more that the ones we forgive. When we choose to hold on to hate and unforgiveness, the baggage we carry gets heavier and heavier.

Some time ago I heard a speaker give a very meaningful illustration about what happens to the load we carry depending on whether we hang on to unforgiveness, or choose to forgive. The illustration was about two groups of people; both groups were wearing backpacks. Whenever someone offended one of them, s/he would drop a rock into his/her backpack. One group of people struggled under heavy loads, their faces showing the effects of hanging onto hatred, while the other group walked with a spring in their step and a look of contentment on their faces. When they were asked to explain the difference in their deportment, the happy group explained that their backpacks had holes in the bottom so that every time they dropped a rock into their backpack, it fell right through. In this way, they acknowledged the hurt, but chose to let it go so that it didn't hinder their walk through life.

We often think of forgiveness as an exclusively Christian concept but even secular psychology has realized the importance of forgiveness for emotional health. When we choose not to forgive someone, the result is often bitterness and resentment which can erode the peace and sense of well-being that we all long for. These emotions are like poison to our soul and spirit. Hebrews 12:15 tells us, "See to it that no one comes short of the grace of God; that no root of bitterness springing up causes trouble,...". Unforgiveness is sin, and all sin hurts us emotionally and often has a negative effect on our physical health as well.

But forgiveness is a very misunderstood concept by many people. Christians often feel that they need to forgive quickly and accept their offenders back into their good graces and be in relationship with them immediately. Non-Christians often feel it is their responsibility to hold grudges and feel bitterness for those who have hurt them, believing they are holding the offender accountable through unforgiveness. Neither of these reactions is biblical, nor will they necessarily result in improved relationships.

Because forgiveness is such an important step in gaining emotional and physical health, we need to examine it in detail. Forgiveness is original with God and He has given us guidance in His Word about its importance.

WHY MUST WE FORGIVE?

It is important to forgive others because God says we must. In Ephesians 4:32 we read, "And be kind to one another, tender-hearted, forgiving one another, even as God in Christ forgave you."

Colossians 3:13 says, "…bearing with one another, and forgiving one another, even as Christ forgave you, so you also must do." In these verses we are not only instructed to forgive others, we are reminded that the reason we are to forgive is because we have been forgiven much by God.

Secondly, it is important to forgive others, because the Bible makes it clear that if we do not forgive others, neither will God forgive us. Matthew 6:14-15 warns, "For if you forgive men their trespasses, your heavenly Father will also forgive you. But if you do not forgive men their trespasses, neither will your Father forgive your trespasses." Mark 11:25 gives us the same message when it says, "… if you have anything against anyone, forgive him, that your Father in heaven may also forgive you your trespasses."

Thirdly, we should forgive others because forgiveness heals us by releasing us from bitterness, resentment and a desire for revenge. As healthy individuals, we are able to maintain healthy relationships and work to restore damaged relationships.

Assertive people find it easier to forgive others because they have a healthy self-esteem. When we have a healthy self-esteem, we know that we didn't deserve the hurt that was inflicted on us, and our sense of self is not threatened by what happened to us. We also realize that if we allow ourselves to carry a grudge against the person who has hurt us, we will be the ones to suffer because every time we relive the offense in our minds, we will feel the original pain while the offender walks freely. To prevent this, an assertive person will address the issue and seek to restore the damaged relationship.

A passive person usually has a somewhat low self-esteem and as a result, their sense of self is threatened. However, they will not do anything about resolving the damaged relationship. Instead, they will nurture critical thoughts and possibly avoid contact with the person who has offended them.

Aggressive people also have a poor self-esteem and feel that to salvage their dignity they need to seek revenge by retaliating, or at the very least, hold onto unforgiveness. A passive/aggressive person will strike back in devious ways which cannot be directly traced back to them.

WHAT SITUATIONS CALL FOR FORGIVENESS?

One of the best examinations of the whole topic of forgiveness is Lewis Smedes' book, <u>Forgive and Forget</u>. In it he points out that we will experience many hurts in life but not all hurts will require forgiveness on our part. This is because some of these hurts will come to us simply because of our vulnerability to hurt in various situations. While many of these hurts will be unfair in the sense that we did nothing to deserve them, yet when there is no one who purposely caused that hurt, there will be no need to forgive anyone. We will simply need to recognize that life was never promised to be fair and we need to take our lumps the same as anyone else without expecting specialized treatment to protect us from all hurt in life.

Smedes says, "I will offer three examples of unfair hurts deep enough to bring us into a crisis of forgiving: *disloyalty, betrayal,* and *brutality.*" He goes on to explain that disloyalty is, "… when I belong to a person and I treat him or her like a stranger." P.33 We should be able to count on loyalty from our family and to a lesser degree from our friends. When they let us down, they have treated us like a stranger according to Smedes.

If our family member or close friend goes one step further and begins to treat us like an enemy, they have not only been disloyal, they have betrayed us. And finally, Smedes says, "We are brutal whenever we reduce another person to less than human excellence. It may be violent rape. It may be a degrading insult. Brutality, no matter who commits it, confronts us with one of the most agonizing crises of forgiveness." P.37

In the counseling office, we meet with many people who have been deeply hurt. Sexual abuse is one of the major reasons a person will seek counseling. When this abuse has come from a father, grandfather, uncle, brother, sister, or cousin, all three deep hurts of disloyalty, betrayal, and brutality have occurred.

When a little child is sexually molested by a family member or a friend whom she trusted, she will have trouble sorting through her feelings about the incident. Even when children are very young, they instinctively know that something is very wrong while the abuse is happening. The child has been taught in the past that this relative could and should, be trusted. Now there is confusion and fear. This fear is preyed upon by the relative when the child is threatened that something bad will happen to her or her family if she tells what happened.

The child will have difficulty expressing rightful anger when in the past she felt only love and trust for this person. When this child goes to Sunday School and Church, she hears that she should forgive those who have hurt her so she may bury her confused feelings and try to be happy even though her fear grows every time the abuse continues, or even when the abuser visits their home. That brings us to the next question:

HOW DO WE GO ABOUT CHOOSING FORGIVENESS?

Just how do we go about choosing forgiveness? As was stated earlier, Christians are sometimes prone to forgive quickly, taking the offender back into their circle of relationships. In our counseling office, we see danger in forgiveness that comes too quickly and that ends in bringing the offender back into the relationship too soon. Sometimes the relationship should never be restored if it would bring more abuse. This is especially true for sexual abuse victims.

These victims will need to forgive in order for healing to take place, but first they will need to work through issues carefully. One of the first things a sexual abuse victim, or a victim of any offense, needs to do, is to be honest about their strong emotions about what has happened. Anger, shame, hurt and fear are some of the emotions that victims feel; emotions that need to be resolved.

As mentioned earlier, the Bible does not forbid us to be angry, but it tells us not to sin in our anger, and not to stay in our anger. A sexual abuse victim needs to acknowledge his or her anger and validate the right to feel this way. Righteous anger says this should never have happened and every effort will be made to prevent it ever happening again.

Journaling can be one way of validating feelings. It also helps the victim to defuse some of the strong feelings in a healthy way. Another benefit of journaling is helping victims to clarify what issues are important to discuss when he/she chooses to confront the offender. When the victim does have the opportunity to confront the offender, they will be able to clearly enunciate what happened, why it was wrong, and that he requires an apology and changed behavior. In asking for a change in behavior the victim is setting new boundaries for any future relationship.

Journaling can also help sexual abuse victims put the blame for the abuse in the right place. When incest takes place some children feel a degree of pleasure along with the pain and shame about what is happening. This is simply because our bodies are programmed to react to certain stimuli. The young child however, doesn't know what to do with these mixed feelings. Due to the fact that they felt some pleasure, they may feel that they are to blame for the abuse and this increases their feelings of guilt and shame. Journaling can help a person describe what happened in some detail which can help them realize that they were victimized which allows them to let go of these feelings. Now they can choose to forgive their abuser(s).

It is unrealistic to think that one simple act of journaling for the purpose of dealing with the abuse and choosing to forgive, will wipe out all the hurt and anger but it will be a start. I believe we can forgive and that our forgiveness can be genuine, even when some anger remains. Smedes agrees when he says, "The reality of evil and its damage to human beings is not magically undone and it can still make us very mad." P.141 If we allow our anger to be the driving force behind setting better boundaries or protecting ourselves in some other way, then the anger that remains after forgiving is a good thing. It can ensure a better future even though we will have to live with the consequences of what has happened to us. As we move forward in our lives, we will see our anger begin to fade, more and more.

REJECT REVENGE

Anger that won't be satisfied unless we get revenge is not a good thing. We need to be very aware that seeking revenge only keeps the anger burning strongly, leading us to do things that we will later regret. Now we will need forgiveness. An angry client once told me that she had been so angry at her boyfriend that she had driven to his house and thrown one of his gifts right through the front window into his living room; soon after my client received a visit from a police officer. Now she looked like the more dysfunctional one in the relationship and her attempt at revenge only brought her more pain and embarrassment.

Seeking revenge doesn't always require an action; it could be a torrent of words that come out of our mouths, seeking to hurt our offender as much as he hurt us. The NLV of Psalm 39: 1-3 describes our feelings as we try to control what we say: "I said to myself, 'I will watch what I do and not sin in what I say. I will curb my tongue when the ungodly are around me.' But as I stood there in silence – not even speaking of good things – the turmoil within me grew to the bursting point. My thoughts grew hot within me and began to burn, igniting a fire of words." What a clear description of what happens when we allow ourselves to speak hastily, without curbing our tongue; this fire of words can do a lot of damage!

We also need to realize that revenge never evens the score; instead "...revenge locks us into an escalation of violence. ..." says Smedes, "The only way out is forgiveness." He points out that revenge cannot even the score since "...no two people, no two families, ever weigh pain on the same scale." P.168

COALS OF FIRE

In the NIV of Romans 12:19-21 we read, "Do not take revenge, my friends, but leave room for God's wrath, for it is written: 'It is mine to avenge; I will repay,' says the Lord. On the contrary: 'If your enemy is hungry, feed him; if he is thirsty, give him something to drink. In doing this, you will heap burning coals on his head.' Do not be overcome by evil, but overcome evil with good."

This Scripture is demonstrated in a rerun of "The Waltons", a TV show about the Walton family during the 1930's. The parents demonstrate an important lesson with regard to forgiveness. In this episode a travelling book salesman, Mr. Reid, writes up a book order for Mrs. Walton in return for her $3.00 down payment. Instead of sending in the book order, he uses the $3.00 to buy a doll for his little girl who will be having a birthday soon. When the Waltons allow him to sleep in their barn and join them for meals, they are "…pouring coals of fire…" on the salesman's head even though they had learned about his duplicity. While John Boy was ready to confront the salesman in a somewhat aggressive way, Mr. Walton stopped him and continued to provide opportunities for Mr. Reid to come clean. When the salesman did not confess what he had done and made preparations to leave, Mr. Walton confronted him in private. Even then, Mr. Reid was not about to make amends; he declared he was going to give the doll to his little girl and it didn't matter to him who had paid for it. Again, Mr. Walton extended grace and let him depart with the doll that their money had purchased. Before the episode ended, Mr. Reid's conscience caught up to him, he returned the doll and brought the $3.00 down payment back to Mrs. Walton.

Returning "good for evil" doesn't always end with the offender doing the right thing; this is a T.V. show where every problem needs to be resolved in one hour. In real life we may have to wait much longer for an offender to do the right thing and sometimes they will never do the right thing. It's also important to remember that we should address the issue as Mr. Walton did, and to extend grace when they do not respond in a positive way. Then it will be even more important to set healthy boundaries to protect ourselves from further hurt.

PRAYING A BLESSING ON OUR ENEMIES

There are some situations where we will need to be willing to do good to someone who continues to show contempt for us. Many Christians are suffering persecution from fellow citizens simply because they are Christians. We know this is happening in many third world countries but it is happening here as well, only in more subtle ways. It's possible that in the situation in which our son Randy found himself, he was being picked on especially because he is a Christian.

Forgiving is the first step; next we should consider blessing those who have hurt us by praying for them and doing good to them in other ways. This does not negate the need for boundaries; even the Waltons told Mr. Reid he was not welcome when he first returned. Choosing to forgive and blessing our offender may result in unexpected blessings for us. If their conscience never convicts them and they never do the right thing, that is not our responsibility. The Bible encourages us to bless others and pray for them; in Matthew 5:44 we read, "But I say to you, love your enemies, bless those who curse you, do good to those who hate you, and pray for those who spitefully use you and persecute you."

In I Peter 3: 8-9 we are exhorted to "... be of one mind, having compassion for one another; love as brothers, be tenderhearted, be courteous; not returning evil for evil or reviling for reviling, but on the contrary blessing, knowing that you were called to this, that you may inherit a blessing."

This is not easy to do; we know how hard it is because we needed to pray for God's blessings on the people who had hurt us in the incident that we related earlier in the book. When we pray blessings on our offender in obedience to God, the biggest change happens in us; we cannot continue to harbor resentment and bitterness in our hearts for someone that we are asking God to bless.

LAYERS OF FORGIVENESS

The layers of forgiveness are related to the severity of the offence. We often face slight offences many times a day, depending on how much we are relating to others in a day. When someone cuts in front of me on a busy street, I may feel annoyed but I'm not likely to relive the incident over and over and harbor bitterness for the other driver. My ability to forgive and forget would be relatively easy. If, however, his careless driving caused me to have an accident which resulted in extensive damage to my vehicle, or put me in a wheelchair, the level of forgiveness necessary would be much deeper.

Forgiveness is a process and as we move through this process, we are moving through the layers of forgiveness. The first time that I make a choice to forgive someone of a serious offence, it is strictly an intellectual decision; there will likely be no warm feelings associated with the decision. When we are reminded again about the offence and experience painful emotions, we need to choose once again to forgive and refuse to feed our hurt by seeking revenge or nurturing negative emotions.

Every time we repeat the process of choosing to forgive our offenders, we go to a deeper layer of forgiveness. In some situations we do regain the ability to have warm, loving feelings towards our offender. Reconciliation may, or may not, happen even then.

As mentioned earlier, I would agree with author Paul Williams that while forgiveness is mostly in the hands of the victim, reconciliation is mostly in the hands of the perpetrator. If the perpetrator acknowledges his wrong doing and makes the necessary changes in his behavior, it will improve the chances of a reconciliation happening. I believe the victim would still have the option of moving towards reconciliation or remaining distant; this, in spite of having chosen forgiveness.

GOOD FROM EVIL

As Christians we need to know that God doesn't waste anything that happens in our lives and He has the ability to bring good out of evil. Referring again to the situation that led to our relocating to another city and province, the negative events that precipitated our move, has, in the long run, become a blessing. The need for a Christian counseling centre in the new city was much greater than the previous city. This allowed us to establish our office with much support from the churches in the city, support that continues today.

Joseph, whom we talked about earlier as someone who had a positive attitude in looking for solutions rather than concentrating on problems, could also attest to the fact that God can use a negative event to bring about a positive situation. If Joseph had not been in Egypt to organize the storage of grain in the years of plenty, he would not have been able to save the lives of his family during the time of famine. The Genesis 50:20 principle is one that we should remember even before we see the end results. In other words, when someone sins against us we need to realize that God can bring good out of this and focus on looking for this good rather than feeling sorry for ourselves. Genesis 50:20 in the New Living Translation says, "As far as I'm concerned, God turned into good what you meant for evil…."

FORGIVE AND FORGET?

Forgiveness does not mean forgetting. A sexual abuse victim will never forget that the abuse happened; other traumatic abuses will also be hard to forget. Therefore, we should not equate forgiveness with forgetting.

The Israelites were actually encouraged to remember and Smedes calls this "redemptive remembering". They were not to remember or relive the difficult things that had happened to them in the past; they were to remember "…the miracle of survival and renewal."p.174 In Exodus 12: 25-27 the Israelites were reminded, "When you arrive in the land the Lord has promised to give you, you will continue to celebrate this festival. Then your children will ask, 'What does all this mean? What is this ceremony about?' And you will reply, 'It is the celebration of the Lord's Passover, for he passed over the homes of the Israelites in Egypt. And though he killed the Egyptians, he spared our families and did not destroy us.' Then all the people bowed their heads and worshipped."

Smedes summarized by saying, "Redemptive remembering drives us to a better future, it does not nail us to a worse past."p.174 This is what Joseph did when he realized why God had brought him to Egypt.

FORGIVENESS AS A RESULT OF ADDRESSING ISSUES

In Luke 17:3-4 we read, "Take heed to yourselves. If your brother sins against you, **rebuke him**; and if he repents, forgive him. And if he sins against you seven times in a day, and seven times in a day returns to you, saying, 'I repent,' you shall forgive him."

We can see from these verses that it is important to confront someone who has offended us. I believe that when we confront someone as soon as possible after the offense has occurred, we enable forgiveness and reconciliation to happen much more quickly than if we keep quiet and try to deal with the hurt on our own. There will be times when we find that we are hurt due to a misunderstanding and by addressing our hurt, the misunderstanding can be cleared up and reconciliation can take place.

Addressing the issue can also be beneficial for the offender; he may not have realized that his behavior was hurtful. When we bring it to his attention, he may change his behavior, preventing further hurt to ourselves or to others. When we choose to forgive someone, we will indeed, "inherit a blessing", the blessing of God's favor and sometimes the blessing of a deeper relationship with the person who earlier offended us.

A little quote in the Daily Bread, published by Radio Bible Class, sums up forgiveness well, "Getting revenge may make you even with your enemy, but forgiving him puts you above him."

Today I was reading Matthew 18:35 NIV where we read, "This is how my heavenly Father will treat each of you unless you forgive your brother from your heart." I wondered about the phrase, "from your heart", what exactly does this mean? Perhaps it relates to the fact that sometimes we can say that we forgive someone but then we bring up old issues of hurt again and again. This would demonstrate that we have not really forgiven "from the heart". It doesn't mean that we should never think about the offense again but we should not bring it up to the offender as a reminder of what they have done. When we bring up old issues, we are behaving in a passive/aggressive way, wanting the offender to hurt a little more even though we have assured them of our forgiveness. It would indicate that we either want them to "hurt" a little or that we would even want them to do something special to make up for their offense. Once we have addressed the issue and by an act of the will, chosen to forgive, we need to leave the issue behind us.

Forgiveness is a decision, an act of the will; it is not a feeling. We may still feel the hurt of the offense, but now the only person we can safely talk to about the issue is God. Even then, we need to purposely put the issue behind us so that it will no longer hurt us. We need to focus instead on what God wants to accomplish in us, using everything that comes into our lives, both pleasant and hurtful.

FORGIVENESS, BOUNDARIES AND RECONCILIATION:

While it is vital to forgive others, we must be careful not to assume that forgiveness means reconciliation. In some situations, reconciliation will be possible due to the genuine remorse, apology, and restitution.

In other situations, we need to make a choice to forgive our offender, but we need not reconcile with this person if it is not safe to do so. This is most often the case when sexual abuse has occurred. If reconciling would put the person in danger of receiving more abuse, we would discourage it. Choosing not to be in relationship with someone is one way of setting a boundary.

The healthiest relationships are those in which we respect the other person's boundaries and we ask them to respect our boundaries.

What exactly is a boundary? In simple terms, a boundary is letting others know what you will and will not, put up with. It can be as simple as letting someone know that you do not want phone calls after a certain time of the evening. When your children were young, you may have set a boundary for them with regard to coming into your bedroom; you may have asked them to knock before entering as a way of respecting your privacy.

More important personal boundaries are the ones that relate to how people treat you and speak to you. Earlier we talked about the Silver Rule which says, "Don't let anyone do to you what you wouldn't do to them." Remembering this rule can help you in setting boundaries. If someone is treating you with disrespect either with their actions or their words, you need to address it, letting them know you are not happy. You also need to let them know the changes you would like to see, and let them know what the consequences will be if they continue the unacceptable behavior. If the change is not forthcoming, we may choose to end that relationship. Most of the time people will respect us for being assertive, and they will change their behavior.

In our office we will often send home the set of videos by Cloud and Townsend, simply called Boundaries. They have also written a book and a workbook that help people work through their own boundary issues. We highly recommend that you look into watching these videos and working through the workbook if you have boundary issues in your life.

Jesus set a boundary for the woman caught in adultery; her story is found in John, chapter 8. We read about how her accusers bring her to Jesus, telling Him that she was caught in the very act of adultery. Jesus simply told them that the man without sin should throw the first stone at the woman. After her accusers slunk away, one by one, Jesus told her, in verse 11, "Neither do I condemn you; go and sin no more."

In layman's language, Jesus was saying, "I forgive you for what you have done, but I don't want you to continue in your sinful ways. Go and live a life of purity."

* * *

The four personalities handle conflict differently; when necessary or possible, the assertive person will address the issues and try to come to a resolution. If the offense requires the justice system to become involved, they will trust justice to prevail.

Aggressive people will seek revenge in hurtful ways, having allowed their anger to turn into resentment, bitterness and even hatred. Passive/aggressive people incorrectly feel that holding onto hatred keeps the offender accountable and they determine never to let go of their hatred. I have had clients who simply stopped coming for more counseling sessions because they were not willing to forgive those who had hurt them. As a result many of these clients were not able to move forward in their lives; first they would need to let go of the hatred and bitterness in their hearts.

ACCEPTING FORGIVENESS:

While looking at the topic of forgiveness, we also need to look at the fact that many times, we find it difficult to accept the forgiveness that God offers to us. As a result, we walk around with a heavy heart, full of condemnation and self-hatred.

Romans 8:1 says, "There is therefore now no condemnation to them which are in Christ Jesus." When we hold onto our guilt and self-condemnation, we are in effect, saying that our ability to punish ourselves is more valuable than the death of Christ on the cross. This of course, is not true and we need to let go of our guilt and accept God's forgiveness.

Some of our clients have expressed the idea that holding onto guilt is what will keep them from re-offending. This is not true; we are more likely to stay away from sinful behavior by recognizing how much God loves us than by feeling guilty and worrying that we will sin again. Feeling guilty keeps us focused on the sinful activity and may even cause us to sin again; we may get discouraged and decide that since we feel guilty, we may as well do something for which we will truly be guilty.

PENANCE:

In this day and age, it's hard to understand that there are still some people who feel that in order to be forgiven, they need to do penance. Many years ago when Wes was in Real Estate, he went to someone's home to list it for sale, but no one came to the door. Eventually, he heard a woman call out that she was in the basement, and that he should use the back door. He went in and found her huddled over a fire she had built in a five-gallon pail, with blankets hanging around a small area in the basement.

Wes was shocked to find her is such dire circumstances; it was in the dead of winter with the temperature around minus 30 degrees. All the water and plumbing pipes had frozen and the electricity had been cut off. Wes assured this elderly woman that she didn't need to live this way; he volunteered to call Social Services and get the heat back on in her home.

Instead of gratitude, this woman shouted "No! I'm doing penance. I've committed a grievous sin and I need to do penance. Don't call Social Services!"

We may not do something as drastic as this woman did, but when we hold onto guilt that God has already forgiven, we are basically doing the same thing.

I believe it was Bill Bright who wrote some little books on important topics of the Christian life for Campus Crusade, who introduced me (Martha) to the idea of "Spiritual breathing". I embrace this concept whole-heartedly and practice it.

The basic idea of spiritual breathing is that the moment we realize we have sinned by having an ugly thought about someone, speaking unkind words, or sinning with our actions, we need to ask God for His forgiveness. This confession is like breathing out the carbon dioxide of sin. Immediately, we need to breathe in the fresh oxygen of God's forgiveness. Others have called this "keeping short accounts with God". We do not need to wait until a special time or be in a special place; we can deal with our sin as soon as the Holy Spirit convicts us.

This can be a very private moment between God and us, unless of course, we have overtly sinned against someone and we need to apologize to them and make amends where needed.

* * *

Monica needed to deal with the whole area of forgiveness; she still felt guilty for abandoning her sister Julie and she felt some resentment towards her parents for their poor parenting. She knew it was time for her to contact her family and deal with her feelings of resentment, as well as to ask for their forgiveness. She dialed her old home number and found that it still worked; her family must still be in the same house in the city that she had left five years ago.

She waited while the phone continued to ring; finally, the answering machine kicked in and she heard the message. As

Monica listened to her mother's voice on the machine, her heart began to ache. Her mother's voice sounded like she was hung over or high on drugs; how could she go back to her childhood home? Monica almost hung up before leaving a message but she changed her mind and left a message, letting her parents know that she would be coming home to visit in two weeks.

In the weeks that followed, Monica wondered if her parents would return her call, telling her not to come. Would they be home when she arrived; if they were, would they be hung over? In spite of her feelings of dread, Monica loved her parents and her sister, and now that she had made plans to go home, she was anxious to get there.

The day of Monica's two week vacation from her job, finally arrived. She had packed a small suitcase the night before so in the morning she quickly showered and dressed, then left for the bus depot. Once there, she bought her ticket and walked onto the bus.

It would be a three hour bus ride, giving Monica a lot of time to think about what she would find at home. She knew she needed God's strength to face her parents so she pulled her Bible from her purse and began to read in the Psalms. David certainly knew fear while running away from Saul but he always looked to God for strength and protection; Monica wanted to do the same.

By the time the bus pulled into the station, Monica's emotions had been all over the place, but now she sensed a deep peace that God would be with her in this place as He had been with her in the past five years.

As she stepped off the bus and looked around, she saw no one that she knew; suddenly she was nearly knocked off her feet by someone from behind. Her sister Julie had thrown her arms around her and when Monica turned around, she returned the embrace.

Monica was amazed at the beautiful young woman she saw before her. Julie, at seventeen, was tall and slender, and her auburn hair was arranged in a style that suited her somewhat angular face. But the best part of seeing Julie was her big welcoming smile and her eyes which sparkled with excitement.

It was almost noon so Julie suggested they go to a local diner for a bite to eat before going home. It was here that Monica found out that Julie had moved out on her own two years ago but since she kept in touch with her parents, they had told her that Monica was coming for a vacation.

They spent some time catching up about the details of their individual lives. Monica found out that Julie was doing very well. She was living on her own, working part time, and finishing high school. She checked up on her parents at least once a week because they were still getting high on drugs or alcohol.

Monica pushed away her plate and reached out to take Julie's hands, looking very serious. Julie squeezed Monica's hands and asked, "Why so serious? Let's enjoy this time together!"

"I do want to enjoy our time together Julie," replied Monica, "but first I need to apologize to you for leaving home the way I did; basically abandoning you to parents who were not very responsible. I should have stayed to look after you. I'm so sorry. Can you forgive me?"

Julie replied, "I have to admit that when you first left, I was very angry. But it also made me realize that our parents were never going to be the parents I needed, so it would be up to me to take care of myself. From that time on, I looked for every opportunity to earn some money and save enough to move out as soon as possible."

Julie went on to explain how she had done odd jobs and when she was fifteen, she got a part time job which allowed her to move out on her own. She admitted that it had been hard and that in fact, it was still hard, but she was happy to be on her own.

Julie squeezed her sister's hands again and assured her, "Of course I forgive you. It doesn't sound like your life was all a bed of roses either, but we'll both make it."

Monica stood and gave Julie a big bear hug. When she let go, she sighed and said, "Now for the hard part. How do you think mom and dad will react to me coming home after all these years?"

Julie shrugged her shoulders and replied, "I think they'll be happy to see you, but if they're drunk or high on drugs, it'll be anybody's guess."

The girls hopped on a city bus and ten minutes later they got out at the stop half a block from their parent's home. Neither of them spoke as they walked the short distance to the house, but both were wondering what was waiting for them inside.

Julie knocked on the door; when no one came to open it, she turned the knob and finding the door unlocked, she went inside, pulling Monica with her.

"Look who I found!" she called out. Her parents emerged from the back room and came to greet the girls. Monica hugged her parents; both parents smiled somewhat sheepishly, and gave her a weak hug in return. Julie was due at work for the afternoon and evening shift so she left Monica alone with their parents.

Again Monica spent some time letting her parents know about some of her life experiences since she had left home. In asking about their lives, she realized there was not much to hear; they had done very little to improve their situation. They were still struggling to make ends meet and using the few resources they had to buy drugs or alcohol.

Monica's stomach was queasy but she knew she should do what she had come to do. She asked her parents to sit together on the sofa and pulled her own chair up close. Then she told her parents, "I came because I miss you and wanted to see you, but I also came because I need to talk to you about some serious issues."

Monica told her parents that for years after leaving home, she had harbored resentment towards them. She had felt anger at them for their addiction to drugs and alcohol which had prevented them from giving her and Julie the care and attention they had needed.

Monica told them that she had accepted Jesus as her Savior and she had been able to talk through a lot of her issues with the pastor at the church as well as the director of the youth center. She had also realized that she needed to forgive her parents for their lack of good parenting. Monica told her parents that she needed them to know how hard their addiction had made life for her and Julie, but that she was choosing to forgive them.

Monica went on to say, "I'm also here to ask for your forgiveness. It was wrong for me to leave the way I did, abandoning you and Julie, and never calling until two weeks ago. Can you forgive me?"

Her parents nodded weakly and were about to get up and walk away but Monica stopped them. She continued, "There's just one thing more. I appreciate your forgiveness and I'm choosing to forgive you, but I would like both of you to get some help. Will you do it?"

Her father retorted, "Help? With what?!" Monica's heart sank; she realized her parents were still in denial about their addictions. Monica replied, "If only you would admit you have a problem and go for help, life would be a lot happier for everyone."

Monica's mother lashed out at her, "It's fine for you to get all religious, going to church and talking to that pastor, but don't think you can come home and tell us what to do! Dad and I enjoy life just fine!"

Monica had made reservations at a local hotel and she left her parents soon after with a heavy heart. In the next week Monica made short visits to her parents' home every day, but she spent most of her time with Julie. They even discussed the idea of moving in together some day.

On one of her visits to her parents' home, her mom suggested that to show that she was really sorry for leaving home, she should move back and start caring for them. Sadly, Monica shook her head and replied, "When neither of you admit to having a problem, and you refuse to go for help, I can't move home and let you carry on with your addictions. I'm sorry but it won't happen as long as you're in denial.'

Before leaving for home, Monica shared with Julie what had happened at "the club" and how this had led her to the church where she had given her life to Christ. She shared with Julie how God can use even the most difficult things in life to draw us to Himself. Monica assured Julie that she would pray for her, for God's protection and guidance in her life, and that she too, would come to know God personally.

With a final wave to Julie, Monica boarded the bus and was on her way.

* * *

When Monica asked her parents for their forgiveness, she also asked them to go for help. In this way she was letting them know what she wanted from them. She also set a boundary by refusing to move home as long as they remained in denial and were not willing to get help.

* * *

Louise was much too passive to confront Tom about his abusive behavior. She blamed herself for the problems in their marriage, yet she struggled with resentment towards Tom. She didn't get help for herself, nor did she set any boundaries about how Tom treated her. Whenever Tom would complain about something she had done, Louise begged for his forgiveness.

* * *

Jack's low self-esteem led him to believe that in order to preserve his dignity, he needed to control everyone in his circle of family and friends. He felt confident only when he could be in charge of his circumstances, and since this is impossible for anyone, he often flew into a rage, blaming everyone but himself for what happened. Controlling what others do is not what it means to set boundaries; when we set boundaries we are attempting to protect ourselves, not to hurt others. Jack felt he would be showing weakness if he would ask for forgiveness or extend forgiveness to others.

* * *

Samantha was a typical teenager who didn't respect the boundaries of her mother or even her friends. Her mother had asked her again and again not to eat her snacks in the living room but Samantha continued to do so. Samantha's mother worked full time and her evenings were busy doing the laundry, cooking, and other household chores. She explained to Samantha that eating in the kitchen would help to keep the living room tidy and lessen the workload for her.

Samantha continued to take snacks into the living room and when her mother pointed out the crumbs on the carpet, she would quickly mumble, "Sorry". Experience taught her mother that Samantha wasn't really sorry; she hoped that with maturity things would eventually change.

Chapter V
CAUTIONS IN RELATIONSHIPS

Ellen was new to the church but she wanted to get involved; being a bench warmer had never been her style. One Sunday morning she picked up a brochure at the church which outlined the many different areas of ministry and discovered that the church had a group that was involved with the arts. From the write-up in the brochure, it looked like this group of people organized art work to decorate the sanctuary for special events. This sounded like the perfect area for her to get involved. Ellen was an artist and it pleased her to see the church recognizing art as a gift from God.

Ellen called the group leader and went to a planning meeting the very next week. She thoroughly enjoyed being involved in the group, not only because she could use her artistic talents, but also because she enjoyed the camaraderie she was beginning to feel with the rest of the people involved. When her husband broke his leg at work and finances were tight while he was off work, she found a lot of support within the group.

One morning, Ellen opened up her computer to check on her email account and was surprised to see that Lindsay had sent her an email. Ellen didn't know Lindsay well; she was the quiet member of the group so she opened the email, wondering what Lindsay might have to say. She was surprised to see that Lindsay had written a lengthy letter full of details about an abusive past and complaining that the church wasn't doing enough to help her. She ended her essay with an appeal to Ellen for help with finding a job.

Ellen felt bad for Lindsay but she also felt that Lindsay was being unfair in her criticism of the church. She knew of several people who had received financial help from the church and she also knew that the pastoral care team visited people in hospitals and offered counseling for others dealing with difficulties in their life. Besides this, Ellen knew that she could not get involved in personally ministering to Lindsay; her severe arthritis meant that she needed to look after herself.

Ellen sent a warm response to Lindsay by email, assuring her of prayer support, but letting her know that she could not help in any other way at this time. The response from Lindsay was quick and sharp. She informed Ellen that she had believed that as women who loved the Lord, they were to be there for each other. She let Ellen know that she had lost respect for her.

Thankfully, Ellen knew that this nasty reply came from someone who believed she was entitled to be cared for as a victim. Ellen also knew that she couldn't allow herself to feel guilty; she knew her limits and they didn't include helping Lindsay at this time.

WE NEED EACH OTHER:

I came across an illustration many years ago which points out the importance of inter-dependence in a marital relationship; it can also apply to other relationships.

In the illustration we can let our two hands represent the two people in a relationship. The finger tips on each hand represent the strengths of each person while the space between the fingers represents the weaknesses of each person. When the two hands push against each other with their finger tips, they will have a very tenuous relationship, always vying for dominance; if someone tries to break up the relationship, they will likely be successful. If however, the finger tips on each hand cover the weaknesses on the other hand as when we fold our hands in prayer, then we have a much stronger relationship. This makes it harder for others to break up the relationship. If we wrap a cord around the two hands, the cord representing God, the relationship becomes even stronger. Ecclesiastes 4:12 in the NLV tells us, "A person standing alone can be attacked and defeated, but two can stand back-to-back and conquer. Three are even better, for a triple braided cord is not easily broken." In other words, we need each other. We all have different strengths and weaknesses and when we do what we can for ourselves and for others, and we accept help from others in our areas of weaknesses, we are being inter-dependent. With God binding our relationship together, both people in the relationship will benefit.

MUTUAL MINISTRY:

Helping others and receiving help from others is a good way to deepen our friendships. Most churches are realizing the value of small group gatherings; these groups are sometimes called Cell Groups, Care Groups, Home Groups, or Life Groups. These groups basically become the church in a smaller setting which allows the members of the group to get to know each other well enough to share freely their joys and their struggles, and to ask for prayer support. It can be within this group that accountability can be practiced as well.

At one time we belonged to a small group where three different members asked for prayer support in their effort to stop smoking. They knew it was bad for their health and that God would want them to care for their bodies by stopping this destructive habit. The group was non-judgmental but they did ask these people every week about their progress. Sometimes phone calls were also made outside of the regular meeting times to assure these fellow believers of their support.

In another small group we have experienced real bonding due to serious health issues in almost all the families represented in the group. Four of the couples in this group have grown even closer in their relationship and they have come together to anoint an individual with oil and to pray for his healing. We have seen God answer prayer in that the gentleman with cancer is now in remission. We continue to trust God for healing in two other situations where the illness is a severe case of depression.

CODEPENDENCE:

But helping others is not always done with the right motives. People who do not have a healthy self-esteem and who are not assertive will sometimes help others out of an unhealthy need to be seen as a good person. Often they will anticipate a need and begin to help others without waiting to be asked. This can sometimes be a good thing; however, this same person may wonder why others don't anticipate their needs and offer help without being asked. When this help doesn't come, the do-gooder may become resentful, yet he has no one to blame but himself. This is codependent behavior.

What exactly does it mean to be codependent? In her book, Codependent No More, How to Stop Controlling Others and Start Caring For Yourself, Melodie Beattie says that "A codependent person is one who has let another person's behavior affect him or her, and who is obsessed with controlling that person's behavior." She goes on to say, "But, the heart of the definition and recovery lies not in the other person – no matter how much we believe it does. It lies in ourselves …" p.36 Beattie sums it up when she says, "It is not good to take care of people who take advantage of us to avoid responsibility. It hurts them, and it hurts us. There is a thin line between helping and hurting people, between beneficial giving and destructive giving." P.94

I would encourage you to read Melodie Beattie's book for more information on codependent behavior and how to change this behavior.

Codependent behavior can be explained with the Karpman Drama Triangle as observed by Stephen B. Karpman. This behavior can be something simple like being at a big family gathering and Sally notices that the sink is piled high with dirty dishes. As a codependent person, Sally will fill the sink with hot, soapy water and start washing the dishes. By doing this, she is going up one side of the triangle, rescuing lazy family members who always try to get out of doing the dishes. She may feel that she is doing the dishes to truly help out, but often the motive is to win approval from other family members.

Soon Sally's role changes to that of victim when no one seems to notice her good works. No one had asked Sally to do the dishes, she didn't have to do them but she did. Now she is moving down the other side of the triangle, feeling sorry for herself and feeling angry at her family for what she is doing. A healthy person might say, "Well, that's all for me! Someone else can take over!" Sally however, will probably keep on washing dishes and with each swipe of the dishcloth, she may think angry thoughts about her uncaring family. Now she is completing the bottom of the triangle, feeling used and abused.

A more serious situation is when we do something for another person that they really need to do for themselves, or when what we do, enables unhealthy behavior or prevents growth in the other person. When the wife of an alcoholic calls his work place to say that her husband has the flu when he is really nursing a hangover, she is enabling her husband's bad behavior. By protecting her husband from his boss' anger, she is assuming the role of rescuer. When this happens repeatedly, the wife will become resentful and take on the role of victim. Since she has rescued him before; her husband assumes she will continue to call the boss for him and in the end she gets angry at her husband and feels used and abused. However, since she is not assertive enough to confront her husband about his behavior, nothing will change in their relationship.

We know of a father who has allowed his son, a drug addict, to come back home and live there free of charge, even bringing his drugs into the house. It would seem that this father is codependent; perhaps he needs the love and approval of his son so much that he actually enables his son's immature behavior. By allowing his son to stay in his home without paying rent, the son is not growing up and taking responsibility for his own housing needs. Further, by allowing his son to do drugs in his home, the father is encouraging this behavior which will destroy the son if he does not get help. This situation demonstrates the thin line between helping and hurting someone. In this case, the father may feel he is helping his son when in reality, he is hurting him.

The bottom line is that when we help others out of genuine love our relationships are deepened. When helping comes out of a self serving need, the friendships rest on a shaky foundation with at least one person watching carefully to determine if the other person is fulfilling his or her needs.

MARGINS:

Having margins refers to setting limits around how busy we allow ourselves to become. This is very important so that we can fully enjoy the things in which we invest our time, energy and money. If we get involved in too many areas, we feel fragmented and cannot do our best work in any area. As Christians, we often feel that we don't have the right to say "No" to any task we are asked to assume in the church. If we are passive, people-pleasers we will have more difficulty in saying "No". It takes an assertive person who feels confident enough to risk upsetting someone with their "No" to set healthy margins for themselves. When we can say "No" we also have the time and the freedom to say "Yes" to the things that God is asking us to do. If we try to juggle too many responsibilities at once, we may actually lose everything.

As assertive persons, we will realize the importance of learning to love and accept ourselves. We will also realize the importance of carving out some private time for ourselves each week. In our office, we provide our clients with a one week calendar page with each day divided into three parts. We then ask clients to fill in the spaces with the different responsibilities that fill these spaces each week. Very often we find that our clients have not left any spaces free for leisure time. We will suggest that they need to offload some responsibilities to leave 3 – 5 spaces free for unplanned events or for time to nurture themselves.

A funny story can help us understand this concept. Wes' brother-in-law wears a toupee which is important to note for this story. One very windy, stormy day, Ken and his wife Irma, stopped for coffee at a local convenience store. Irma waited in the car while Ken went to purchase two cups of coffee. As he came back across the parking lot, the wind threatened to remove his toupee. Without thinking, Ken reached up to hold onto his hair, spilling hot coffee on his head; he jerked his hand back, spilling even more coffee. The wind gave another hard tug at the toupee so Ken reached up with his other hand, spilling the second cup of coffee. Having let go of the toupee, it now lifted off completely and began rolling along in the parking lot. Completely disgusted, Ken threw both cups of coffee to the ground and hurried after his toupee, catching it just before it got caught in some thistles at the edge of the parking lot. "I didn't want coffee anyways!!" said Ken, as he climbed back into the car, giving Irma a dirty look as she tried to hide her snickers behind her hand. Because Ken tried to juggle both cups of hot coffee and still protect his toupee, he nearly lost everything. When he was willing to let go of the coffee, he was able to save his hairpiece even though it was badly soiled.

The illustration may be very inadequate, but we can apply it to our lives in this modern day world where everyone seems to be on a merry-go-round that is spinning faster and faster. An assertive person has much better time management skills than a passive or an aggressive person; they are able to prioritize activities in order of importance for the health and well-being of themselves and their families.

We have a good model for setting margins in Exodus 18:13-23. This is where we read about Moses who was leading the Israelites out of the land of Egypt to the Promised Land. The Israelites were bound to be in conflict with one another at times; they also had questions about God's laws. Since Moses was their leader, he "...sat to judge the people; ...from morning until evening." When his father-in-law, Jethro came to visit, he said, 'The thing that you do is not good. Both you and these people who are with you will surely wear yourselves out.' Jethro then suggested a plan whereby Moses would choose some able, God-fearing men whom he would train. These men could then handle the less difficult problems and bring only the really difficult ones to Moses. He encouraged Moses, "If you do this thing, …then you will be able to endure, and all this people will also go to their place in peace."

MATURITY:

Relationships run much smoother when the people in a relationship are mature. As we have been examining the meaning of assertiveness, we see that thinking, speaking and acting assertively, is a mature way of behaving.

The problem is that there are a lot of immature people in this world and we need to examine whether we are among them. Scott Peck in his book, Further Along the Road Less Travelled, says that, "…most people who look like adults are actually emotional children walking around in adult's clothing." Peck has another book called, The Road Less Travelled; I believe even those titles inform us that not many take this road, the road that leads to maturity.

The Bible has much to say about the importance of growing up into maturity. Ephesians 4:13b says, "until we all reach unity in the faith and in the knowledge of the Son of God and become mature, attaining to the whole measure of the fullness of Christ.". Verse 15 says, "…speaking the truth in love, we will in all things grow up into him who is the Head, that is, Christ.".

I Corinthians 14:20a says, "Brothers, stop thinking like children." And I Corinthians 13:11 says, "When I was a child, I talked like a child, I thought like a child, I reasoned like a child. When I became a man, I put childish ways behind me."

All of these Scriptures emphasize the importance of growing up. God's desire for each one of us is to grow as Christians so that we become more like Christ. That will mean a mature way of relating to other people in our sphere of relationships.

Immaturity leads to selfish and dysfunctional ways of relating to others.

Ephesians 4:14 says, "Then we will no longer be infants, tossed back and forth by the waves, and blown here and there by every wind of teaching and by the cunning and craftiness of men in their deceitful scheming." This implies that immature people allow others to influence them too much; they do not have the self confidence to make their own decisions, based on God's Word whenever possible, and stick by them. In trying to please others, they choose to let others control their emotions and actions.

Maturity also means that we recognize that life will not always be easy; we will experience pain and difficulty in our lives. We will also have to deal with immature people along the road of life. It is unrealistic to think that we will only have to deal with other mature people.

Pain is often a part of our life that helps us to grow up and become mature. But while pain will always be a part of our experience in life, we should not go looking for pain; that would serve no purpose. A martyr might look for pain, believing that simply experiencing pain is heroic; pain must have a purpose and many times the purpose of pain is for our spiritual growth.

Again in Further Along the Road Less Travelled, Dr. Scott Peck says, "...what characterizes most immature people is that they sit around complaining that life doesn't meet their demands....But what characterizes those relative few who are fully mature is that they regard it as their responsibility—even as an opportunity—to meet life's demands."

The passive person will not make many demands of life but they may give up the hope that they can be successful or have an enjoyable life. When the passive person is being treated badly, they may continue to accept this treatment, believing they have no choice but they will feel very sorry that life has dealt them such a miserable hand.

The aggressive person will definitely demand that life should meet their needs and wants; if this comes at the expense of pain for others, they are not concerned, they care only about themselves. They will act superior to others in an effort to convince themselves of their own self-worth.

The passive/aggressive person will engage in devious activity to get what they want in life; when they get what they want they may not enjoy it, knowing they have acted in a very self-centered way.

It is the assertive person who recognizes that life does not always hand us an easy road but they also recognize that the struggle to overcome difficulties is part of the maturing process. This is especially true for the Christian. When we are going through difficult times, we lean heavily on God and on the prayers of our fellow Christians. When we come out on the other side of the difficult situation, we often look back at this time as having been a very special time in our life. We may have sensed a real strengthening from God and we realized that it was during this time that we grew in maturity.

As mature people we see ourselves as God sees us, and we treat others as equals. The most important benchmark against which we should measure ourselves, is checking to see if we are becoming more like Christ every day. Romans 8:29 says, "… God knew his people in advance, and he chose them to become like his Son, …"

I've heard it said that in the west we ask God to remove the burdens from our back while in the east, people pray that God would strengthen their backs so they can carry their burdens. To me, the eastern way of praying represents more maturity.

CHOICES:

In summarizing the value of assertiveness with regard to relationships, we need to conclude this section by talking about the importance of making choices. Just as we have a choice in what our attitude or behavior will be, we can make choices about our relationships. Assertive people can decide whether they want to initiate new relationships, or stay in present relationships. Assertive people can also terminate some relationships that are draining us of energy or joy, or that tempt us to do things we would not normally do. They can also make choices about the depth of the relationship.

Assertive people will see the value of choosing other healthy, assertive people with whom to be in relationship. Recently a couple came for counseling where one of the issues they needed to resolve, was their tendency to drink too much. As Christians, we need to support one another and one of the recommendations I gave them, was to develop friendships with healthy couples who would support them in their desire to curb their drinking.

This is not to say that we should never associate with non Christians; we are to be "salt and light" in this world, drawing others to a relationship with Jesus. However, our closest relationships should be with healthy people who can challenge us to grow and we can do the same for them.

Everyone has the ability and opportunity to make choices; sometimes our choices will be very limited, nevertheless, we will still be able to make a choice.

While it is important to choose relationships that will encourage and support us, we can also choose to accept the imperfections in others, even when they cause some pain. We should not try to avoid all relationship pain but recognize that the support we get from others can outweigh the pain.

Recently I read a fable of the porcupine in an email which is a good way to sum up the value of relationships even though they can be painful at times. I'd like to relate it here for you.

Fable of the Porcupine

It was the coldest winter ever – Many animals died because of the cold. The porcupines, realizing the situation, decided to group together. This way they covered and protected themselves, but the quills of each one wounded their closest companions even though they gave off heat to each other.

After awhile, they decided to distance themselves one from the other and they began to die, alone and frozen. So they had a <u>choice</u> to make: either accept the quills of their companions or disappear from the Earth. Wisely, they decided to go back to being together. This way they learned to live with the little wounds that were caused by the close relationship with their companion, but the most important part of it, was the heat that came from others. This way, they were able to survive.

The best relationship is not the one that brings together perfect people, but the best is when each individual learns to live with the imperfections of others and can admire the other person's good qualities.

* * *

Monica made the choice to leave home and look for a better life. It didn't happen immediately, but in time, she did experience a more fulfilling life.

Louise was very afraid to make a choice that would give her a better life, but eventually, she did move in with her son and daughter-in-law, and begin proceedings for a legal separation.

Jack made many unhealthy choices in the way he treated his co-workers, not really caring about their welfare.

Samantha made a very selfish and hurtful choice by accusing her mother of abuse, and choosing to go to the concert with her friends against her mother's wishes.

So we can see that assertive people have healthier relationships and when assertive people are also Christians, they will have even more reason to treat others with the respect that Jesus asks of us in Luke 6:31 where we read. "Do to others what you would want them to do to you."

Part IV

ASSERTIVENESS DEEPENS OUR RELATIONSHIP WITH GOD

Grace was an appropriate name for the young missionary who had returned from her mission assignment in Burundi to enjoy some rest during her furlough. She loved the people of Burundi and was quick to extend grace to them, even when they totally misunderstood some of the things she was trying to do for them. She also extended grace to her family and friends who didn't understand why she would waste her young life on people who didn't seem to want help. Grace extended grace to the Mission Board who had asked her to take only a partial furlough because they didn't have enough staff to cover her duties for a whole year. Yes, Grace extended grace to everyone it seemed, everyone that is, except herself.

The Mission Board had a policy that all missionaries attend some mandatory counseling sessions while on furlough to work through any issues that had come up while on the field. Grace ended up in our office and after seeing the results of some psychological testing, it was obvious that she struggled with a low self-esteem and a passive personality.

Grace not only struggled with a low self-esteem, she actually hated herself! During one of her sessions, she admitted that she felt like God must view her as a pile of manure, totally unworthy of His love! Grace had sacrificed so much to serve God, giving up a comfortable life at home to go to a strange country with people whose language she couldn't understand, and whose customs were hard to learn. Yet Grace was willing to do this because, as a passive person, she needed to please the Mission Board. She hoped that by going she would also gain the approval of God since passive people depend on performance-based acceptance, even though her home church taught grace.

She would go to Burundi to share the love of God with these people yet Grace had not truly understood or accepted the love of God for herself! Our hearts ached for Grace and thankfully the Mission Board allowed her to remain at home and get the necessary counseling so that before she returned to Burundi, we saw a new glow on her face and a spring in her step.

* * *

Throughout the earlier chapters of the book we have referred to what the Bible says about the different topics. In this section of the book we want to go into more depth about how the different personalities affect our relationship with God.

Chapter I
THE BIBLICAL VIEW OF OUR RELATIONSHIP WITH GOD

There is another way that we could use the triangle illustration. We could look at the section all across the bottom of the triangle as being our relationship with God. Having a personal relationship with God is what gives us a firm foundation for everything else that we do in our lives. With this foundation, we can build a solid, healthy inner life, which then helps us to reach out to other people in healthy relationships.

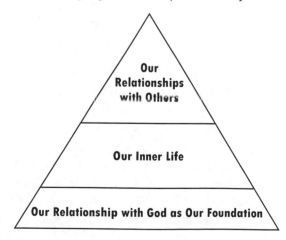

When all three aspects of the triangle operate in a healthy way, we feel complete; as a whole person, we can enjoy the abundant life offered to us in John 10:10.

The most important thing the Bible tells us is that God loves us so much that he desires a personal relationship with each one of us; God made this relationship possible by sending His Son Jesus to earth to live with mankind and to die for us. We talk often about the fact that Jesus died for us but do we really stop to think what it really meant for Jesus to give up His home in heaven to come down to earth to be with us, to identify with us, to know what it means to be human?

Hebrews 4:15 tells us that Jesus was fully God and fully man. As a man, Jesus experienced every temptation that we face; this fact gives us comfort but it wasn't easy for Jesus any more than it is for us. Jesus was abused physically, emotionally, psychologically, spiritually and sexually. This may sound like an outrageous statement, but think with me for awhile. No one doubts that Jesus suffered horrendously during His trial and His death on the cross. But during Jesus ministry on earth, He was criticized and rejected by many people; this is emotional and psychological abuse. It must have hurt when, "He came unto His own and His own received Him not." John 1:11 KJV. We read more of the details of his rejection in Matthew 13:53-56:

> When Jesus finished teaching with these stories, he left there. He went to his hometown and taught the people in the synagogue, and they were amazed. They said, "Where did this man get his wisdom and this power to do miracles? He is just the son of a carpenter. His mother is Mary, and his brothers are James, Joseph, Simon, and Judas. And all his sisters are here with us. Where then does this man get all these things?

> So the people were upset with Jesus. But Jesus said to
> them, "A prophet is honored everywhere except in his
> hometown and in his own home." So he did not do
> many miracles there because they had no faith.

No rejection is pleasant, but when our own family rejects us, it
hurts with a deeper hurt that is hard to accept.

Jesus predicted that all the disciples would abandon Him and
when Peter declared, 'Even if all fall away, I will not.' Jesus
rebuked him and described to Peter how he would deny his
Lord three times even before the rooster would crow twice. This
is exactly what happened and even though Jesus had predicted
it, it must have hurt Him afresh to hear Peter follow through
with his denial. Peter wasn't the only disciple who rejected
Jesus; Judas was the first disciple to reject and betray his Master.
Judas was disappointed in Jesus and became his enemy. He
went to the religious leaders and offered to betray Jesus into
their hands for a fee. Later, Judas realized what a terrible thing
he had done and he threw the thirty pieces of silver into the
temple, and went and hanged himself. Mt. 27:5.

Jesus also felt the effects of spiritual abuse by the religious
leaders of the day. Jesus taught about the things of the heart
that really matter while the religious leaders of the day were
more interested in legalistically requiring everyone to perform
outwardly according to the letter of the law, while overlooking
the more important matters. In Matthew 23 Jesus confronted
them:

> "How terrible it will be for you teachers of religious
> law and you Pharisees. Hypocrites! For you are careful
> to tithe even the tiniest part of your income, but you
> ignore the important things of the law – justice, mercy,
> and faith. You should tithe, yes, but you should not

> leave undone the more important things. Blind guides!
> You strain your water so you won't accidentally swallow
> a gnat; then you swallow a camel!" (vv23-24).

Obviously the religious leaders didn't appreciate the teachings of Jesus which challenged their authority, so in Matthew 21 we read how they, in turn, questioned Jesus' authority to teach the things he was teaching in the temple. Again in Mark 8 we see the Pharisees asking Jesus for a miracle with the express purpose of trapping Him. And when Judas came back to them, admitting that he had betrayed an innocent man, the religious leaders answered," 'What is that to us? That's your problem, not ours.'" Then we read, "So what Jeremiah the prophet had said came true: 'They took thirty silver coins. That is how little the Israelites thought he was worth….'" Mt.27:9NCV.

We too, need to take seriously Jesus' words and question ourselves: "Are we outwardly performing in ways so that no one can find fault with us, while at the same time harboring bitterness, resentment and unforgiveness in our hearts?"

And finally, when Jesus hung on the cross with only a loin cloth, Jesus was experiencing sexual abuse. In the days when Jesus was on earth, men were dressed with long mantles over tunics and a belt. If someone was wearing only an undergarment (tunic & belt), they were considered to be naked. (From a site called JESUS CENTRAL.com). It was a disgrace even to lift the hem of their cloak to be able to move faster; therefore, hanging on the cross, almost completely exposed, would have been considered very inappropriate, except for common criminals. Jesus was indeed, counted among the two thieves who hung on either side of him.

Verbal abuse was also used against Jesus. Even while he hung on the cross, "… the leaders laughed and scoffed. 'He saved others,' they said, 'let him save himself if he is really God's Chosen One, the Messiah.' The soldiers mocked him, too, by offering him a drink of sour wine." Luke 23:35-36 NLT

Yes, Jesus knows what it is like to suffer abuse but he was willing to do this to make a way for us to become a member of God's family. In John 14:6 Jesus said, "'I am the way, the truth, and the life. No one can come to the Father except through me....'" You and I deserve to die for our sins; the worst sin being the sin of rejecting Jesus as our Savior. Romans 3:10 tells us that "There is none righteous, no, not one." and 3:23 agrees, "For all have sinned and fall short of the glory of God." This means we are all in trouble and Romans 6:23 reminds us that "...the wages of sin is death,...". However, the verse goes on to say, "...but the gift of God is eternal life in Christ Jesus our Lord." When Jesus died on the cross, He took the punishment of death to pay the wages of our sin; we simply need to acknowledge our sin, ask God for forgiveness, and invite Jesus into our life. When we accept Christ, we receive eternal life and we can look forward to spending eternity with God but more than that, we can have a personal relationship with God the moment that we accept His forgiveness and begin to live for Him.

I (Martha) was the third child born to parents who had been raised with a religious background that depended heavily on legalistically obeying a specific set of rules. Most of these rules were man-made with some connection to the Bible. When I was around five years old, some wonderful people from an evangelical church in a town about fifteen miles from our acreage, came to our home every Sunday afternoon to have Sunday school with us. They encouraged us to invite our nearest neighbors to attend as well. While someone was having a Bible lesson with the adults in the house, other people taught the children in the big outdoors. Occasionally, we would be asked to put on a little program for the adults. This was my first exposure to the Gospel.

After a few summers of coming to our home, this group of people encouraged us to start attending their church in the town. We did that and I looked forward to the sense of longing for God that came along with spending time at church. God's Spirit was obviously drawing me to Himself because I would often be very emotional during a service. When I was almost nine years old, I was allowed to attend the summer camp program for children put on by this church. I say "allowed" because the age limit in those years was actually nine but because I would turn nine before the summer was over, I was approved to go as a camper. I was also "allowed" to go by my parents; with seven children, money was very tight and I do remember one summer when only some of the siblings were able to attend camp due to a shortage of funds.

That first year at camp would turn out to be pivotal for me in my spiritual life. While the games, crafts, and Bible lessons were most enjoyable, the pivotal moment came for me when three girls cornered me in a hallway of the girls' dormitory. They asked me if I was a Christian; I replied that I didn't know. Undeterred, they proceeded to ask me if I wanted to be a Christian. Although I wasn't sure exactly what that meant, I knew that it was what I wanted so I said, "Yes". With that, the girls led me down the hall to meet with one of the counselors who shared John 3:16 with me:

> For God so loved the world that he gave his only begotten son that whosoever believeth in him should not perish, but have everlasting life.

The counselor led me in a prayer to invite Jesus into my life. It was evident even during the rest of that week that the Holy

Spirit was at work in my life, helping me to further understand that I was now a child of God, having a personal relationship with Jesus. I will be forever grateful to those three girls and I know they will get their reward in heaven, regardless of how unorthodox their method of evangelism.

Wes' experience was quite different. He likes to say that he literally had the hell scared out of him. His parents were not Christians when they married but they did accept Christ in the early years of their marriage and starting attending an evangelical church when the children were still young. Being the oldest in the family, Wes had been to Sunday school often enough to know that Jesus had died on the cross for him and that he needed to invite Christ into his life. Being young, he felt no urgency to make a decision for Christ until that pivotal day in his life.

Living in a small town, his family was allowed to have a barn on their property; this barn had fallen into disrepair and it fell to Wes, aged 12, to climb up on the roof to repair it. Beside the barn was a power pole with a transformer on it. Wes was intent on finishing the repair job before the impending rain storm; he did notice that the sky was rapidly turning dark and occasional flashes of lightning lit up the sky so he hurried all the more.

All at once a huge flash of lightning struck the power pole and transformer, splitting the pole in two and setting the transformer on fire! Wes felt the reverberations throughout his whole body, and knowing he was not ready to die, he knew just what to do. He jumped off the roof, ran into the house, and asked his mother what he needed to do to make sure that heaven would be his home in eternity. His mother led Wes in a prayer asking Jesus to come into his heart and be his personal Savior.

Both Wes and I are grateful for the opportunity we had to begin a personal relationship with Jesus at an early age. We have had many years to nurture this relationship and we are blessed that in our counseling office we have the privilege of sharing Christ with many of our clients. We will not impose our faith on anyone but we do share our firm belief that if Christ is the foundation upon which we build our lives, our marriages, and in fact, all of our relationships, will be healthier and happier.

Having a personal relationship with God is the most important relationship we can have in this world but how we think about God and how we think about ourselves will make a difference in the kind of relationship we have with God. Assertiveness can help us to have a healthy relationship with God; likewise, a healthy relationship with God can help us to be assertive. The assertive person can accept God's forgiveness and have a much deeper relationship with Him than someone who is Passive or Aggressive. An assertive person will be far more likely to hear God and understand and accept his love.

Unfortunately, many people miss out on the joy of a close, personal relationship with God because they feel unworthy to be loved by God. We learned earlier that assertive people develop a healthy self-esteem while passive, aggressive, and passive/aggressive people, have a low self-esteem and feel unworthy of God's love. This was the case with the young missionary, Grace.

Secular society teaches us that in order to be acceptable we must perform perfectly; when we do, we will get that gold star which the kindergarten teacher gives out sparingly, we will be asked to the prom by that strong, handsome football star of the High school, and we will get those sought-after promotions at work.

Secular society is not alone in promoting performance-based acceptance; many cults or even evangelical churches teach the importance of striving for absolute perfection in how we live our lives. As mentioned earlier, many churches become very legalistic about outward appearances and actions, while accepting sinful attitudes.

Recently I was with a small group of women who were attending an introductory course to the Christian life. A shy woman waited for some time before she began to share her experiences of being brought up in a very strict sect of the church. This woman shared how much of their life revolved around the church, being forced to go to meetings almost nightly with three day meetings on some weekends. She shared how she had never felt like she was good enough; as a result, she found it hard to accept the love of God. She is very thankful to have found a church that teaches about God's grace, but she still wondered out loud, "Maybe if I improved my life, I would find it easier to accept God's love."

The sad thing about striving for perfection is that it never works; only God and Jesus are perfect. When we realize that we cannot be perfect, we sometimes rebel and move in the opposite direction entirely. Again, this same woman shared that when her parents finally realized they needed to leave this church, her father started to sin with a vengeance. He purposely did everything that he was forbidden to do while in the church, even leaving her mother and marrying another man! It was only God's grace that brought this wonderful woman to a church that showed her God's unconditional love and acceptance. She enjoys a personal relationship with God but the nagging thoughts about needing to try harder, are difficult to erase from her mind.

Perfectionism causes problems in many areas of our lives, but especially with regard to living for God. Since we realize very early in life that we are far from perfect, we struggle with a poor self-esteem. Having a low self-esteem causes us to hesitate to enter into a vital relationship with God; we feel unworthy to enter His presence through prayer and when we read the Bible we are convicted about our lack of perfection so it is easier not to read it at all. When we have missed the mark we often beat ourselves up, unable to accept God's love and forgiveness. We often have the impression that we need to "clean up our act" before God could ever love us or want us to be his child. This is a lie of the enemy of God, Satan.

Erwin Lutzer, in his book, <u>HOW TO HAVE A WHOLE HEART IN A BROKEN WORLD</u>, shares the testimony of a sexual abuse victim who said, "He (Jesus) wanted to love the real me, not the counterfeit I tried to offer Him and everyone else." Well said! In trying to be strong and not showing our brokenness, we are really rejecting Jesus. And then we wonder why Jesus is not helping us to heal.

We see this in our office. One of our clients who was sexually abused when she was only six has suffered the consequences of this abuse throughout her young life. She is now in her twenties and has achieved an appearance of a very confident, assertive young woman. The truth is that she is hurting deeply, feeling betrayed by God himself. She feels he should have prevented the abuse and since he didn't, she's afraid to trust him for anything else, especially her healing. Admitting her brokenness is too frightening for her; she needs to maintain control to prevent any further abuse. Unfortunately, maintaining control also means that she is not taking a leap of faith to accept Jesus and trusting him for healing as well as eternal life. She feels safer in her own ability to be in control even though she has intellectually realized the validity of the Christian faith. Jesus wants to love the real broken and hurting young woman, not the counterfeit strong, self-assured woman that she presents to everyone. This client is doing what many of us do when we are broken and hurting. We take our brokenness to God, asking Him for healing, only to snatch the problem back to ourselves, not allowing God to heal us and to use this difficulty in our lives to teach us new things.

Once we have accepted Christ as our personal Savior, we have the power of the Holy Spirit to help us live the Christian life. This does not mean that we will live this life perfectly, never sinning again. However, when we sin, we simply need to ask God to forgive us and accept that forgiveness. The hard part is accepting God's forgiveness. We are so disappointed in ourselves for sinning again that we find it difficult to believe that God could forgive us. Once again, it is Satan who wants us to focus on our unworthiness so that we wallow in our sorrow instead of accepting God's forgiveness and living in the freedom of his love, free from sin and guilt.

Again, Erwin Lutzer says in his book, "To have a whole heart in a broken world, we must be reconciled to God by accepting the gift of salvation through Christ. But the next step is to know how to keep spiritually clean by accepting Christ's cleansing every single day. A basic axiom is that we tend to repeat sins we feel guilty about. That's why the cleansing of the past is so necessary for victory in the future." P. 13 and on p.14 he says, "Guilt leads to failure, failure to more guilt." This is why we must accept God's forgiveness and not allow Satan's condemnation to lead to such guilt that we give up and sin even more. Feelings are very fickle; we deserve to **feel** forgiven, but we can make a **choice** about which feelings we will accept. We need to learn to trust the fact that God has forgiven us the moment we confess our sin.

In our office, we encourage the use of positive self-talk; we need to affirm that God has forgiven us and whenever the guilt feelings come back, we need to thank God for his forgiveness rather than beg for forgiveness for the same sin over and over.

As a young woman, I knew all about this struggle; it was very hard to forgive myself when I had failed God in some way. As a result, I would ask for forgiveness again and again instead of accepting God's forgiveness. One day God made it very clear to me that dwelling on my unworthiness was exactly what Satan wanted me to do. If he could keep me discouraged about living for God, I would be unable to focus on serving God.

Philippians 3:13 & 14 have become favorite verses and I enjoy sharing them with clients who are struggling with the same issues. These verses come to us from Paul where he says,

> "I don't mean to say that I have already achieved these things or that I have already reached perfection! But I keep working toward that day when I will finally be all that Christ Jesus saved me for and wants me to be. No, dear brothers and sisters, I am still not all that I should be, but I am focusing all my energies on this one thing: Forgetting the past and looking forward to what lies ahead, I strain to reach the end of the race and receive the prize for which God, through Christ Jesus, is calling us up to heaven."

I love it when God gives me a "light bulb" moment; those moments become a part of me. That is not to say that I never struggle with beating myself up, but for the most part I practice spiritual breathing (explained in an earlier chapter), by confessing my sin and accepting God's forgiveness immediately. That frees me up to move forward with a clear conscience to experience intimacy with God, thanking Jesus for His sacrifice for me, and trusting the Holy Spirit to keep my conscience tender.

Something that has been helpful for me is to understand the difference between **condemnation** and **conviction**. Whenever we feel **condemned**, we can be sure our guilt is coming from Satan who is "the accuser of the brethren". Rev. 12:10. The Holy Spirit on the other hand, gently **convicts** us of sin that needs to be confessed and points out the changes that need to happen. Erwin Lutzer further explains the difference between the Holy Spirit and Satan when he writes, "The difference is that the Holy Spirit always points out specific unconfessed sin; Satan always brings to mind sins already confessed or gives us a vague, undefined sense of guilt."

God wants us to enjoy the "abundant life" which includes freedom from guilt. John 8:32 says, "And you will know the truth, and the truth will set you free." As we believe the truth that God has forgiven our sins, we can experience abundant life, free from guilt.

In parts I & II we discussed the importance of our thoughts, attitudes, and emotions, and how this affects our self-esteem and our interpersonal relationships. Now we want to look at how these things affect our relationship with God.

We've explained previously that our thought life determines our moods, and our moods affect our words and our actions. Our thought life affects our relationship with God, and conversely, a healthy relationship with God affects our thoughts. When we accept that God loves us, has forgiven us, and sees us as His children, we will begin to see ourselves as God sees us and we will have a healthier thought life. Because we love God and want to please Him, we will also allow the Holy Spirit to point out when our thoughts are not pleasing to God. It is pointless to try to keep our thoughts from God because Psalm 94:11KJV says, "The Lord knoweth the thoughts of man, …"

We need to pray as David did in Psalm 139:23,24KJV, "Search me, O God, and know my heart: Try me, and know my thoughts: And see if there be any wicked way in me. And lead me in the way everlasting." And Hebrews 4:12cKJV tells us that the Word of God "…is a discerner of the thoughts and intents of the heart." When we realize that our thoughts are not pleasing to God and not helpful for our growth, we need to bring "…every thought into captivity to the obedience of Christ,…"II Corinthians 10:5cKJV

It is important to replace those negative thoughts with more positive thoughts as it says in Philippians 4:8, "Finally, brethren, whatsoever things are true, whatsoever things are honest, whatsoever things are just, whatsoever things are pure, whatsoever things are lovely, whatsoever things are of good report; if there be any virtue, and if there by any praise, think on these things."

It is important to remember too, that we are not privy to God's thoughts. Isaiah 55:8KJV says, "For my thoughts are not your thoughts, Neither are your ways, my ways, saith the Lord." When we encounter difficult times that don't make any sense to our finite minds, we need to surrender our ways to God, knowing that He wants what is best for us.

Attitude is so important and as assertive people, we will strive to have positive attitudes for the most part. In our office we deal with a wide variety of people, some people have very positive attitudes, others do not. Attitude affects our healing process; those people with positive attitudes will heal more readily than those with negative attitudes.

Attitude matters to God as well and since assertive people have healthier attitudes than other people, their relationship with God is deeper than for many other people. A positive attitude which includes having an attitude of gratitude and humility is an attitude that we should strive for in order to please God. Conversely, our relationship with God will enable us to have God-pleasing attitudes.

Our attitude regarding sin is very important. We need to recognize that our sin is very offensive to God; the Bible tells us, " And do not bring sorrow to God's Holy Spirit by the way you live…." Ephesians 4:30a NLT. The King James version uses the word "grieve". We can always come to the throne of grace to ask for God's forgiveness when we sin, but it is important that we do not have the attitude that because of God's grace, we can easily sin, then ask for forgiveness. The early Christians wondered about this as well and Paul told them, "Shall we continue in sin, that grace may abound? God forbid…." Romans 6:1b-2a KJV. As Christians, our love for God and gratefulness for all that he has done for us, should be the motivation to have a positive attitude as well as an expectant attitude about Christ's return.

Our self-esteem is formed by our thoughts and attitudes. How we feel about ourselves greatly affects our relationship with God. A passive person has a low self-esteem and when he considers a relationship with God, he often feels that he is not worthy of God's love so he may continue to live without having a relationship with God. If a passive person does accept Jesus as his Savior, he will often struggle with guilt because he finds it difficult to accept that God has fully forgiven him. He continues to experience a lot of guilt which results in a spirit of defeat. Sometimes the passive person will give up the Christian life altogether, believing that he will never have victory over sin. Other passive people continue to struggle in their Christian life, believing that they simply need to try harder.

An aggressive person has a low self-esteem but he feels that he has to come across as confident and self-assured. This often leads him to feel that he shouldn't need God in his life, that to rely on God would be like leaning on a crutch.

The passive/aggressive person thinks he can hide things from God because he is often successful in hiding things from others.

The assertive person has accepted God's evaluation of himself so he has a healthy self-esteem. He is also realistic and realizes that he has done nothing to deserve God's love and acceptance. He thankfully accepts God's love and forgiveness and strives to deepen his relationship with God by spending time in God's Word and in prayer.

Chapter II
ASSERTIVENESS AFFECTS OUR PRAYER AND BIBLE READING

Betty grew up in a very legalistic Christian home. From her parents she was given the impression that the Christian life is all about keeping certain rules. This belief was further impressed upon her young mind when at the age of 13 she was baptized and joined the church. Before being accepted as a member of the church, Betty was required to sign an agreement that as a member of this church she would refrain from smoking, drinking and a number of other evils. In the classes leading up to the baptism and membership service, the pastor stressed the importance of regular attendance at church and Sunday School, Bible reading and prayer.

Betty enjoyed the warm sense of approval and acceptance by the congregation on the day of her baptism and after being officially welcomed as a member of the church, many people came by to congratulate her and encouraged her to grow in her faith.

Betty tried hard to abide by the rules of church membership but it was not easy and whenever she failed to spend at least fifteen minutes in Bible reading and prayer, she carried around a weight of guilt throughout the rest of the day. One day as she finished reading a chapter from the Bible, she looked at the clock and realized she would need to hurry to get ready to catch the school bus. Although she preferred to kneel for her prayer time, she decided she would just have to pray while getting ready. Silently she began to pray as she brushed her teeth and selected what she would wear to school.

All at once Betty realized that she had been repeating a memorized prayer which was really a grace to be said at meal times! Betty was shocked to realize that she had treated her prayer time with such little respect and attention. She was so embarrassed that she gave up praying altogether for a time. She didn't feel worthy to enter God's presence after what she had done!

* * *

Responding to God's desire for a personal relationship with us is only the first step. As with any relationship, some effort is required on our part to deepen this relationship. To do this, it is helpful to engage in some intentional disciplines, things like spending time reading and studying the Bible, praying, and fellowshipping with other believers in church and small group Bible studies. Betty's pastor was correct in emphasizing these spiritual disciplines but the problem arises when we place our faith for salvation in keeping the spiritual disciplines rather than placing our faith in the finished work of Christ.

Hebrews 4:16NIV assures us that God wants us to approach His throne with confidence for we read, "Therefore let us draw near with confidence to the throne of grace, so that we may receive mercy and find grace to help in time of need." Again, in Hebrews 10:19,20NLT we read, "And so, dear brothers and sisters, we can boldly enter heaven's Most Holy Place because of the blood of Jesus. This is the new, life-giving way that Christ has opened up for us through the sacred curtain, by means of his death for us."

An assertive person will accept that these Scriptures apply to him or her while passive people will still be afraid to approach the throne. Aggressive people may address God in derogatory ways as "the man upstairs" and passive/aggressive people will be afraid to be open and honest with God about anything.

Besides being encouraged to come to God in prayer with confidence and boldness, are there specific ways that we ought to practice the discipline of prayer? First of all, prayer is a discipline; we don't naturally talk to God in prayer unless we have developed a prayer life that started out by being disciplined to carve out time daily to talk to God. It helps us to take that time with God when we choose a specific place to have a "quiet time" with God. It also helps to select a specific time when we plan to take that special time with God; when we make it a regular part of our day just like we plan for work, exercise, meal times, and time with our families.

From the time I accepted Jesus as my personal Savoir, I was taught that prayer is something that you do mostly in your devotional time with God. Read a portion of Scripture, meditate on what it means for you, and then spend some time praying, applying God's Word to your life and praying for any needs you have.

It is important to develop the discipline of concentrated prayer and there are some guidelines we can use in our prayer time. Someone has suggested that we use the letters in the word "Acts" as an acrostic to cover the basic things we should cover in our prayers. A stands for adoration; our prayers should focus first on God, praising and adoring Him for Who He is. C stands for confession; we need to come to God, acknowledging our sinfulness and asking Him for forgiveness, for specific sins and perhaps in general, for the sin of not loving God enough. T stands for thanksgiving; we need to recognize that everything that we have comes from God and we need to express our gratefulness to Him. S stands for supplication; the last thing on our prayer list should be the things we want to ask God for. Before we ask for our own needs, we should pray for the needs of others. Another guide for our prayer time could be to use the letters of the alphabet to praise God for his many attributes, attributes that start with every letter of the alphabet.

But prayer is much more than this. The Bible tells us to "Pray without ceasing." I Thessalonians 5:17 KJV. God is always available to us and for many years I have been practicing prayer by crying out to God throughout the day as a need occurred, or as an opportunity for praise arose. Driving down the street and witnessing a beautiful sunrise or sunset is reason enough to simply say, "Thank You God for the beautiful sunset! You are an awesome artist!" At another time in the day when I sit down with a client, even though I may have prayed for all my clients of the day, now as I face my client, I may cry out to God, "Help Lord! I'm not sure how I'm going to address this issue." I have enjoyed talking to God this way; it feels so natural and unstressed; I am free to talk to my all powerful God, Father, Savior, and Friend, whenever, and wherever I am.

John Burke, in his book, <u>Soul Revolution</u> supports praying throughout the day in any and every situation. He says that since we are all talking to ourselves anyways, (the concept of self-talk), "… the goal is to stop just talking to yourself in your head and enter into conversation with the God who created you for himself." P.60

Richard Foster in his book, <u>PRAYER, FINDING THE HEART'S TRUE HOME</u>, begins the chapter on unceasing prayer with the following quote:

> *When the Spirit has come to reside in someone, that person cannot stop praying; for the Spirit prays without ceasing in him. No matter if he is asleep or awake, prayer is going on in his heart all the time. He may be eating or drinking, he may be resting or working – the incense of prayer will ascend spontaneously from his heart. The slightest stirring of his heart is like a voice which sings in silence and in secret to the Invisible. – Isaac the Syrian p.119*

That quote is an exciting thought; to think that the Spirit is praying without ceasing in us. However, I believe we will become more aware of our communication with God when we have been faithful in practicing the discipline of regular prayer.

We should get so comfortable talking to God that we sense His presence with us all day long, every day, wherever we are, and whatever we are doing. When we see a beautiful sunrise or sunset, a prayer of praise for His blessings should rise up to God as readily as we might offer thanks to a friend for something they have done. A prayer for forgiveness, wisdom, protection, or guidance should readily spring from our hearts as well.

There are many other facets of prayer and many different kinds of prayer. One of the best treatments on the topic of prayer is the one mentioned earlier by Richard Foster. I would encourage you to read it, but most of all I would encourage you to spend time in prayer, sensing the nearness of God and enjoying intimacy with Him.

If our thoughts about ourselves are focused on our unworthiness, we will not spend much time talking to God in prayer; rather we will be ashamed to enter His presence. We need to recognize this as a lie from Satan and come into God's presence, humbly accepting His forgiveness and learn to enjoy His presence.

Some of the old hymns have the most wonderful words about our relationship with God. In the song, <u>In The Garden</u>, the author wrote:

> I come to the garden alone while the dew is still on the roses,
> And the voice I hear, falling on my ear, the Son of God discloses,
> And He talks with me and He walks with me, and He tells me I am His own,
> And the joys we share, as we tarry there, None other, has ever known.
>
> He speaks, and the sound of His voice is so sweet the birds hush their singing,
> And the melody that He gave to me within my heart is ringing.
> And He talks with me and He walks with me, and He tells me I am His own,
> And the joys we share, as we tarry there, None other, has ever known.
>
> I'd stay in the garden with Him, though the night around me be falling,
> But He bids me go through the voice of woe; His voice to me is calling.
> And he talks with me and He walks with me, and He tells me I am His own,
> And the joys we share, as we tarry there, None other, has ever known.

I believe this hymn describes the intimacy we can enjoy as we pray "without ceasing" throughout our day, beginning early in the morning and continuing our conversation until night ends our day. It also points to that special time of retreating from everyday tasks to spend time in the garden with God alone. It stresses the fact that our prayer time comes out of a relationship with God where we can talk to God and He talks to us. Are we quiet and listening for His voice or are we doing all the talking? The more we hear God, the more we will recognize His voice. God speaks to people in different ways, but if we're willing to listen, we will hear him and the more we hear God, the more we will recognize his voice.

Another way that God speaks to us is through His Word. The Bible is God's "love letter" to us; it is also His instruction book for life. If we never crack open the Bible and wonder why God doesn't speak to us, wonder no longer. Some people prefer to have supernatural experiences with God; those are wonderful, but why should God meet you in those ways when you refuse to meet Him in the quietness of your home or study, diligently reading, studying and meditating on His Word. When we get familiar with God's Word, the Holy Spirit can take those words from Scripture and remind us of them to convict us of sin or to comfort us when in distress.

Chapter II
ASSERTIVENESS AFFECTS OUR SPEECH AND BEHAVIOR AS CHRISTIANS

An assertive person with a healthy self-esteem is usually a disciplined person and when our confidence comes from knowing who we are in Christ, every area of our life is affected in a positive way. John Burke, in his book, <u>Soul Revolution</u>, says that the root of all our problems is, "Self-centeredness rather than God-centeredness." P.64 We are all so focused on ourselves that it causes a lot of problems. And because we are thinking so much about ourselves, we think others are thinking about us too, especially when we mess up in some way. We're at a social function or some other event where we have said something or done something that we feel embarrassed about. We might go home from that event and relive our embarrassing moment over and over again; sure that everyone else who was at the event is now thinking negative thoughts about us. The truth is that probably not one person at the event is thinking about us; they are thinking about themselves.

Donna Carter, in her book, <u>10 Smart Things Women Can Do to Build a Better Life</u>, says, "When we're 20, we worry about what people think of us. When we're 40, we no longer care what people think of us. When we're 60, we realize no one was thinking about us in the first place." p.89

When we are God-centered, we will think about how God sees us every moment of every day; we will ask God to help our thoughts to be God-honoring which will lead to words and actions that will honor God and be a blessing to others.

God's Word has a lot to say about our speech. Words are very powerful; they can heal us or hurt us. In Job 19:2, Job questions his friends, "How long will you torture me? How long will you try to break me with your words?" As Christians we should use our words to heal rather than hurt. Colossians 4:6 encourages us, "Let your conversation be gracious and effective so that you will have the right answer for everyone."

The book of Proverbs contains numerous guidelines for our speech. The New Living Translation makes these verses very easy to understand and apply to our way of speaking. In chapter 12, verse 18, we read, "Some people make cutting remarks, but the words of the wise bring healing." In chapter 15, verses 1 and 4, we are given advice on how to prevent anger, "A gentle answer turns away wrath, but harsh words stir up anger." And "Gentle words bring life and health; a deceitful tongue crushes the spirit." An assertive person will try to speak wise, gentle words that will bring healing to another person; the passive/aggressive person will use his tongue deceitfully to crush the spirit of another. Again we read in chapter 25:15, "Patience can persuade a prince, and soft speech can crush strong opposition."

Sometimes it is best to use few words or even keep quiet altogether; when someone is really hurting the best thing we can do is to cry with that person. Proverbs 17:27&28 agree, "A truly wise person uses few words; a person with understanding is even-tempered. Even fools are thought to be wise when they keep their mouths shut, they seem intelligent."

James 3:2-10 summarizes the power of the tongue and the importance of learning to control what we say:

> We all make many mistakes, but those who control their tongues can also control themselves in every other way. We can make a large horse turn around and go wherever we want by means of a small bit in its mouth. And a tiny rudder makes a huge ship turn wherever the pilot wants it to go, even though the winds are strong. So also, the tongue is a small thing, but what enormous damage it can do. A tiny spark can set a great forest on fire. And the tongue is a flame of fire. It is full of wickedness that can ruin your whole life. It can turn the entire course of your life into a blazing flame of destruction, for it is set on fire by hell itself. People can tame all kinds of animals and birds and reptiles and fish, but no one can tame the tongue. It is an uncontrollable evil, full of deadly poison. Sometimes it praises our Lord and Father, and sometimes it breaks out into curses against those who have been made in the image of God. And so blessing and cursing come pouring out of the same mouth. Surely, My brothers and sisters, this is not right!!

An assertive Christian will want to use his words to glorify God and to build up "one another". We can glorify God when we use our tongues to worship and praise God with our prayers, our songs, and our very lives. When we talk to others, let's make sure our words are encouraging even when they may need to be challenging as well.

Assertive people are also able to confidently teach others what they have learned. Titus 2:15 says, "You must teach these things and encourage your people to do them, correcting them when necessary. You have the authority to do this, so don't let anyone ignore you or disregard what you say."

Part of this teaching includes sharing the Good News with those who have not yet asked Christ into their lives. We should not aggressively use Scripture to condemn others for their words or actions; instead, we should ask permission to share what Christ means to us. When others see that our actions agree with our words, they may be willing to listen.

This reminds us that our actions should also be assertive and Christ-like. Our actions should be helpful to others and should show Christ to the world by the love we show to one another. We should in fact, be willing to act as servants to one another. In Philippians 2 we are encouraged to have the same mind and attitude that Jesus demonstrated while on earth. John chapter 13 records for us the last supper when Jesus took the servant's role, taking a towel and a basin of water, and began washing the feet of his disciples. As assertive Christians we need feel no shame about taking on this role of a servant; our value remains the same regardless of what we are doing.

As assertive Christians, we will want to be part of a local church body; as Christians we are already part of the larger, universal body of Christ, but it is also important to be part of the local church. In Hebrews 10:24,25NLT we read, "Think of ways to encourage one another to outbursts of love and good deeds. And let us not neglect our meeting together, as some people do, but encourage and warn each other, especially now that the day of his coming back again is drawing near."

Some clients have indicated they feel that this Scripture does not refer specifically to faithful church attendance; they feel that as long as they are getting together with other Christians in some setting, they are obeying God's Word. I disagree with those sentiments especially because when I have questioned people about how often these meetings take place and how they are structured, many times the meetings take place only occasionally and without any structure. We are weak human beings in many ways and unless we discipline ourselves to get together at regular intervals and structure our time together to include Bible reading and prayer, it may not happen, or at best, it may only happen sporadically.

Jesus is our example in this as well. We read in Luke 4:16NIV "He went to Nazareth, where he had been brought up, and on the Sabbath day he went into the synagogue, as was his custom. And he stood up to read." Notice that it was Jesus' custom or habit to go to the synagogue every Sabbath. In Matthew 26:55 and Mark 14:49 Jesus makes reference to the fact that he had been teaching in the temple daily. Most of us are not free to go to church on a daily basis, but we can make it our habit to attend church services on a weekly basis. If we can add to that, attending a small cell group during the week, we will be the ones to benefit.

Our personality will affect our desire to attend church and how we might be involved when we do attend. A passive person might sit near the back of the church, ready to slip out as soon as the service is over. This person may be hesitant to meet others due to being shy, and to get involved would really stretch their limits. An aggressive person might get involved in some aspect of service in the church but they might try to assume leadership and try to change things to better suit themselves, not mindful of what others want. The passive/aggressive person may try to stir up trouble in the group through gossip or by finding fault with the way things are done. The assertive person will strive to be outgoing, helping others to feel welcome at the church. They will recognize that as part of the local church body, they need to be involved in serving. They will be willing to take on a role of assisting others rather than needing to be in charge, yet they will not hesitate to take on leadership roles when they are approached to do so.

The passage in I Corinthians 12:14-26 speaks of the different members that make up the body of Christ. Nicky Gumbel in his book, <u>QUESTIONS OF LIFE</u>, explains this passage well.

> Paul deals with two wrong attitudes. First, he speaks to those who feel inferior and who feel that they have nothing to offer. For example, Paul says the foot may feel inferior to the hand or the ear inferior to the eye (vss.14-19). It is a human tendency to feel envious of others.

> It is easy to look around the church and feel inferior and therefore not needed. As a result we do nothing. In fact, we are all needed. God has given gifts "to each one" (vs.7). The term "to each one" runs through I Corinthians 12 as a common thread.

> Each person has at least one gift, which is absolutely necessary for the proper functioning of the body. Unless each of us plays the part God has designed for us, the church will not be able to function as it should. In the following verses, Paul turns to those who feel superior (vss21-25) and are saying to others, "I don't need you."

> Again, Paul points out the folly of this position. A body without a foot is not as effective as it might be (see

vs. 21). Often the parts that are unseen are even more important than those with a higher profile.

The right attitude recognizes that we are all in it together. We are all a part of a team – each part affects the whole. From Plato onwards, the "I" has been the personality that gives unity to the body. We do not say, "My head has an ache."

We say, "I have a headache." So it is with the body of Christ. "If one part suffers, every part suffers with it; if one part is honored, every part rejoices with it." (vs. 26)

Paul is describing the passive person as the one who feels inferior and the aggressive person as the one who feels superior. The assertive person is the one who recognizes that we are all in it together and seeks to do things which will bring honor to the body of Christ rather than shame. They are also aware that when one part of the body suffers, they need to reach out to the suffering ones to help restore the body of Christ.

THE FRUIT OF THE SPIRIT:

As Christians, part of growing into maturity, is allowing God to develop the fruit of the Spirit in our lives. Galatians 5:22 & 23 says, "But the fruit of the Spirit is love, joy, peace, patience, kindness, goodness, faithfulness, gentleness and self-control. Against such things there is no law." We believe that assertive people display the fruit of the Spirit in their lives much more so than any of the other personalities.

A person who truly **loves**, loves God first and foremost but s/he also values relationships enough to risk addressing issues to improve relationships.

An assertive person has more **joy** than many others because they feel good about themselves and they treat others well. As a result, they have healthy relationships. They also find **joy** in living for God and seeking to please Him in all they do.

An assertive person experiences **peace** as a result of resolving issues in relationships. Assertive people are also willing to become **peace**makers, often helping others resolve their issues.

An assertive person learns to be **patient** with others, realizing that everyone has baggage and they may need time to deal with it in order to become a good friend.

Assertive people are able to show **kindness** to others and to do **good** to those around them. He uses **gentleness** in the way he rebukes someone when necessary.

An assertive person is loyal to his friends, and to God, showing his **faithfulness.**

An assertive person also seeks to be **self-controlled** in how he speaks and acts towards others.

Part V

OTHER ASPECTS OF ASSERTIVENESS

Chapter I
ROOTS OF NON-ASSERTIVE LIVING

If we are not being assertive in the way we live our lives, then we are behaving in a dysfunctional way. It is true that all families and therefore all people are dysfunctional to some degree. This agrees with the Bible that says "There is none righteous, no not one;" Romans 3:10 NKJV. Since the fall when Adam and Eve sinned, we are all born with a sinful nature.

As we mentioned earlier, knowing Christ as our personal Savior helps us to live assertively, and living assertively helps us to live our Christian lives in ways that please God. II Corinthians 5:17 tells us that "... if anyone is in Christ, he is a new creation; old things have passed away; behold, all things have become new." This is a wonderful truth but we must also take heed to what it says in Philippians 2:12,13, "... work out your own salvation with fear and trembling, for it is God Who works in you both to will and to do for His good pleasure." This means we don't sit back and expect God to change us without any effort on our part.

Recently I read a really good explanation of what is meant by "working out our salvation". The author of this explanation likens salvation to the wedding ceremony but in order for the marriage to be successful, the two people in it need to "work out their relationship". In the same way, God accepts us as His children when we accept Christ as our Savior but we need to "work out" our salvation, learning to love God more and live in ways that please Him.

In Ephesians 4:22-24 we read, "... put off, concerning your former conduct, the old man which grows corrupt according to the deceitful lusts, and be renewed in the spirit of your mind, and that you put on the new man which was created according to God, in true righteousness and holiness."

It is important to realize that while old things have passed away and all things have become new, we have a responsibility to do our part to live as new creations. Often we seem stuck in the old ways of thinking, speaking and acting.

We see from the verses above that we need to work out our salvation, knowing that all the time it is God who is giving us the desire and the power to live our new lives. We also need to put off the old ways of thinking, speaking and acting and put on new ways of being.

There are many other Scriptures we could refer to which encourage us to work hard at living a life that pleases God, all the while, realizing that it is not our works, but Christ's death on the cross that secured our salvation for us.

In the Ephesians passage we are reminded that we are to be renewed in the spirit of our minds. This same thought is given to us in Romans 12:2 which reads, "And do not be conformed to this world, but be transformed by the renewing of your mind, that you may prove what is that good and acceptable and perfect will of God."

When we examine the roots of not living assertively, we find that many times clients have accepted Christ as their Savior, they have become new creations, yet they continue to struggle with living like they are still under the old mindset.

This is where some of the work comes in for working out our salvation. Our mind has been convinced that we cannot live life assertively because of things that happened to us in our families of origin, or with other significant people like teachers, pastors, or employers.

In the New Century Version, we read in Romans 11:16, "…If the roots of a tree are holy, then the tree's branches are holy too." I'm taking this verse out of context because I think it says so well what happens in our families of origin. If we are raised in a home that is fairly healthy, we will have a much better chance of becoming a healthy individual, able to live assertively; the reverse is also true.

People that come to us for counseling, often come from homes that were quite dysfunctional. Even a home that is mostly healthy can give some negative messages to the children. Following are two diagrams that illustrate how the messages we received growing up, continue to influence us.

Please be assured that when we look at how some of our families of origin contributed to our dysfunctional living, we are not doing this for the purpose of blaming. This would serve no useful purpose; it is simply so that we can understand where our negative thinking and our negative attitudes first developed. Once we understand the origin, we can work on recognizing that we no longer need to continue in the same mindset.

When you look at the two trees on the following pages, you will notice that the tree roots represent the messages that we received from our families of origin and from school. Our mind is like a computer and therefore our thought patterns are based on how our computer was originally programmed in our childhood. We are told that 75% of our brain is formed by the age of six and by the time we are eighteen, 95% of our brain is formed. Our mind does not know the difference between truth and lies; it only functions on the information it has been fed.

If in our childhood we were given messages that we were only worthwhile if we performed perfectly; if we were not encouraged for our efforts; or if we were even abused, verbally, physically, or sexually, we will believe the lie that we are not valuable. This message becomes the basis of our belief system.

The trunk of the tree reveals the belief system we have adopted. Our belief system is basically how we feel about ourselves, the world, and how we fit into the world around us. When we do not feel valuable, our belief system will cause us to feel insecure; the more insecure I feel, the more I will be threatened by what others say, and I will have a flight or fight mentality.

In the tree tops we can see the results of living by a negative belief system. With a flight or fight mentality, we will either be defensive, wanting to fight for proper recognition, or we will want to flee by withdrawing and not standing up for ourselves at all. Neither way of behaving will help us to feel good about ourselves because we often sabotage what we need and attract what we fear. What we really fear is rejection by others, and yet we will often sabotage relationships with others because if we reject the other person first, we don't have to worry that they will reject us.

Again, if we were given the message that we are only valuable when we perform perfectly, we will become people pleasers, trying desperately to do things that will make others like us. This could lead to doing sinful things just to please the person whose acceptance we are striving to get. When we do our very best and we feel it is still not appreciated, and we are not measuring up, we may feel emptiness. As a result, Satan will often persuade us to medicate our emptiness with drugs, alcohol or pornography. Then immediately, Satan accuses us for doing these things and our self-worth is eroded even further.

If sexual abuse has caused our belief system to see ourselves as damaged goods, we may unconsciously be attracted to unhealthy people who will once again, take advantage of us. As a result we miss out on healthy relationships, believing we do not deserve them.

If there was a lot of fighting in our homes between our parents, using hurtful words or actions, we will not learn how to resolve conflict in healthy ways and we will not respect our parents or siblings. This disrespect often continues on into adulthood. We will also avoid conflict rather than addressing issues assertively or setting healthy boundaries.

Living in a very dysfunctional home growing up will not encourage us to be open and honest with our parents or siblings about our deepest dreams, goals, doubts, fears and guilt. Openness and honesty may even be viewed as a sign of weakness. Job 3:25,26 says, "What I feared has come upon me; what I dreaded has happened to me. I have no peace, no quietness; I have no rest, but only turmoil." We believe that Satan attacks us at our weakest points.

By looking at the roots, belief system and results in dysfunctional homes, we can see that this is a situation where the people in it, are reacting. In other words, the people are reacting by becoming passive, aggressive, or passive/aggressive.

An Unfulfilling Life

Addictions Controlling
Argumentative Act on Feelings
Sabotage what we need
Attract what we fear Dependant

Insecure

Passive or Aggressive

Low self esteem

Abuse in the home

Alcoholism

Criticism

Put downs

Unhealthy Role Models

Results

A Weak Trunk

Negative Roots Lead to

In the second diagram we see what happens in a healthy family of origin. We still have to go to school and what happens there is not always positive but with a safe home to go to afterwards, we can usually deal with it. No home is completely healthy but there is a big difference when the parents love their children and strive their best to bring up the children as healthy individuals who will be able to deal with the harsh realities of life.

In a healthy family, our parents affirm and encourage us which helps us to feel secure and have a mostly healthy self-worth. We will not need to look to others for validation and we will in turn, be able to encourage others and be there for them. With a healthy self-worth we will be attracted to other healthy people and be able to enjoy healthy relationships.

Healthy role-modeling for resolving conflict will cause us to respect them and give us the courage to set healthy boundaries and address issues.

Having observed good communication skills will help us to be able to stand up for ourselves without becoming defensive or withdrawing and losing valuable relationships. We will also feel safe to be open and honest with our parents and later in life, with others, and hopefully with our spouse. Being open and vulnerable deepens our relationship with others and we can encourage each other in working to overcome negative behaviors.

When we see ourselves as God sees us, we will have a healthy self-worth. We know that as humans we still make mistakes but we also know that God forgives us when we confess our sins to him and he helps us to learn from our mistakes. As a result, we are attracted to other healthy people. Proverbs 27:19 says,, "As water reflects a face, so a man's heart reflects the man." When others see us as someone who can feel good about themselves, they are attracted to us as well.

In healthy families, healthy belief systems due to being given healthy messages during our childhood, lead to healthy roots being laid down for us. We then grow up to be proactive, assertive people rather than reacting in negative ways to the things that life deals out to us.

Hopefully the diagrams will be helpful in understanding what has happened in your family of origin.

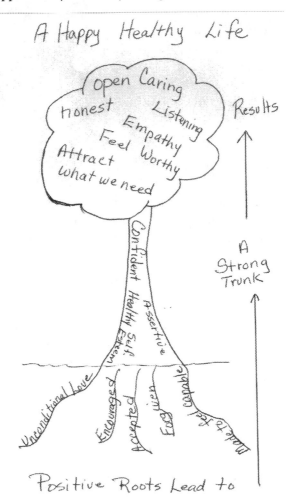

Chapter II
BIBLICAL EXAMPLES OF ASSERTIVE PEOPLE

A. Paul is a good example of a biblical character that was assertive in many ways. Paul had not always been assertive; at one time he had been very aggressive. Before Paul was a follower of Christ, he was called Saul, and he was aggressive in his determination to kill Christians. In Acts 9:1, we read that "...Saul was still breathing out murderous threats against the Lord's disciples." He intended to track down the disciples in Damascus, but on his way, he met the Lord and became a follower of Jesus. Notice the assertive words that Jesus used to confront Paul, combining grace and truth; grace because Jesus called Saul by name and asked him a question, and truth because Jesus named Saul's actions persecution which is what they were.

> As he neared Damascus on his journey, suddenly a light from heaven flashed around him. He fell to the ground and heard a voice say to him. "Saul, Saul, why do you persecute me?"

> "Who are you Lord?" Saul asked.

"I am Jesus, whom you are persecuting," he replied.
"Now get up and go into the city, and you will be
told what you must do." Acts 9:3-6

Paul recognized that Jesus was really the Messiah and
he chose to follow Him rather than persecute Him. Paul
became a "chosen instrument" to share the gospel with
Gentiles. As such, he kept his aggressive tendencies in
check, but he didn't become a passive wallflower either.

Paul demonstrated many characteristics of assertiveness.
First of all, Paul had a positive attitude even in very difficult
situations. There is evidence of Paul's positive attitudes
while imprisoned in a letter he wrote to the Philippians.
Paul's main purpose as a follower of Christ, was to bring
honor to God and to bring the Good News to all people.
This is what allowed him to rejoice that the Gospel was
being spread even more due to his imprisonment.

In chapter one, verses 12-19, Paul wrote that all the soldiers
who were guarding him, knew that he was in chains because
of his faith in Christ. His very life in the prison was a
testimony to God's grace, both to the soldiers and to fellow
Christians who had been emboldened to tell others about
Christ. Paul knew that some people, instead of encouraging
him, were actually preaching the Gospel out of jealousy
and rivalry. Instead of being upset, Paul rejoiced that the
Gospel was being preached, regardless of the motives of
those preaching.

Paul was assertive in his relationships with other people.
In I Corinthians 3 we read how Paul reprimanded the
Corinthians about their lack of growth as Christians.
Instead of berating them in a demeaning way, Paul asked
good questions which helped them to see themselves

clearly. In verse 3, Paul says, "...since there is jealousy and quarrelling among you, are you not worldly? Are you not acting like mere men?..."

By asking questions, Paul hoped the people would examine their behavior and make some positive changes.

In another situation, Paul was very assertive in the way he confronted a fellow Christian and one of Jesus' disciples, Peter. We read about what happened in Galatians 2:11-16. Peter had been eating with the Gentiles before the Jews came, but when they came, Peter separated himself from the Gentiles. Paul accused Peter of changing his behavior to please the Jews who had come. Paul called this hypocrisy and challenged him by asking, "How is it, then, that you force Gentiles to follow Jewish customs?"

Paul also demonstrated the assertive trait of standing up for himself and his rights. There are several examples of this.

Paul and Silas became missionary partners and in Acts 16 we read that they were thrown in prison, after being stripped and beaten. Paul and Silas could have commiserated about their unfair treatment, and allowed themselves to become bitter and resentful. Instead, we read in verse 25, "About midnight Paul and Silas were praying and singing hymns to God,..." Again, Paul and Silas had positive, assertive attitudes and emotions in this difficult situation.

The Lord sent a violent earthquake which caused the prison doors to fly open and loosen everyone's chains. Paul encouraged the jailer not to harm himself; instead, Paul led the jailer and his family to the Lord.

In the morning, the magistrates sent their officers to release Paul and Silas from jail. When the magistrates came to tell them they could go, Paul responded by saying, "They beat us publicly without a trial, even though we are Roman citizens, and threw us into prison. And now do they want to get rid of us quietly? No! Let them come themselves and escort us out." Acts 16:37. In other words, Paul was saying, "They treated us unfairly, let them come and take responsibility for their actions, and treat us right."

Paul knew his rights as a Roman citizen, and he stood up for them; he was not about to slink quietly out of the prison.

In Acts 22 we read about Paul in the middle of a riot in the city of Jerusalem. When the crowd got really riled, the soldiers were commanded to take Paul into the army building and to beat him. As the soldiers were preparing to beat Paul, he asked a nearby officer, "Do you have the right to beat a Roman citizen who has not been proven guilty?"

Paul did not keep quiet nor did he angrily defend himself; he simply asked an appropriate question, which is an assertive action; as a result, he was spared a beating.

Again, in Acts 25:11, when Paul faced Festus in the judgment seat, knowing that he had done nothing wrong, Paul appealed to Caesar. Paul knew, and demanded, his rights.

B. Peter and John were also assertive. In Acts 3, we have the story of the crippled man who was begging by the Temple gate. He had been crippled all his life and people carried him to the gate every day so that he could beg from the people passing by.

When Peter and John came by, they told him they didn't have silver or gold, but they could give him something better. Then, in the name of Jesus, they commanded him to get up and walk.

When the people were astonished and wanted to give glory to Peter and John, they made it clear to everyone that the same God who raised Jesus from the dead, had also healed the man who had been crippled.

They continued to preach boldly that, "...there is no other name that has been given under heaven by which we must be saved."

The Jewish leaders paid attention and were afraid because many were believing in Jesus and following Him. They felt their power slipping, so they called Peter and John in and asked them not to preach about Jesus any more.

In Acts 4:19 & 20 we read how Peter and John were assertive, "But Peter and John answered and said to them, 'Whether it is right in the sight of God to listen to you more than to God, you judge. For we cannot but speak the things which we have seen and heard.'"

Again in Acts 5:27-29 we read, "Having brought the apostles, they made them appear before the Sanhedrin to be questioned by the high priest. "We gave you strict orders not to teach in this name." he said. "Yet you have filled Jerusalem with your teaching and are determined to make us guilty of this man's blood." Peter and the other apostles replied, "We must obey God rather than men!"

It took courage for Peter and John to preach boldly when they knew it would anger the Jewish leaders, and even more courage to assert that they would obey God rather than the Jewish leaders.

In Acts 4:13 we find out why Peter and John were able to be so assertive. We read, "Now when they saw the boldness of Peter and John, and perceived that they were uneducated and untrained men, they marveled. And **they realized that they had been with Jesus.**" As Christians, we have the assurance of being valuable, worthwhile people who can boldly speak out to share the Good News of the Gospel and to stand up for ourselves.

C. David was not assertive in every way but he is a good example of assertiveness with regard to taking ownership of his wrongdoing. When David sinned against God by taking a census of his fighting men, God gave David a choice of punishments. David chose a plague rather than a famine or fleeing from their enemies. In II Samuel 24:17 we read, "When David saw the angel who was striking down the people, he said to the Lord, `I am the one who has sinned and done wrong. These are but sheep. What have they done? Let your hand fall upon me and my family.'"

D. Jesus is the most important example for us; the goal for us as Christians is to become like Christ. Romans 8:29NLT tells us that "For God knew his people in advance, and he chose them to become like his Son, so that his Son would be the firstborn, with many brothers and sisters."

Earlier we talked about how Jesus used questions assertively. In Mark 11:27-33, Jesus used creative questioning to address his opponents. In these verses we read,

> They arrived again in Jerusalem, and while Jesus was walking in the temple courts, the chief priests, the teachers of the law and the elders came to him.

"By what authority are you doing these things?" they asked. "And who gave you authority to do these this?"

Jesus replied, "I will ask you one question. Answer me, and I will tell you by what authority I am doing these things. John's baptism – was it from heaven, or from men? Tell me!"

They discussed it among themselves and said, "If we say, 'From heaven,' he will ask, 'Then why didn't you believe him?' But if we say, 'From men …'" (They feared the people, for everyone held that John really was a prophet.)

So they answered Jesus, "We don't know." Jesus said, "Neither will I tell You by what authority I am doing these things."

The most well-known example of Jesus asserting himself is when he entered the temple and "… began driving out those who were buying and selling there. He overturned the tables of the money changers and the benches of those selling doves, and would not allow anyone to carry merchandise through the temple courts. And as He taught them, he said, "Is it not written: 'My house will be called a house of prayer for all nations.'? But you have made it a 'den of robbers'. Mark 11:15-17

Jesus is also our example of being passive when the need for this arises. Jesus knew that His whole purpose for coming to earth was to die for our sins, and in Acts 8:32 we read, "He was led like a sheep to the slaughter, and as a lamb before the shearer is silent, so he did not open his mouth."

The more we practice being assertive, the more we will be able to discern whether we need to be assertive, or if the situation calls for passivity or even aggressive action.

It is important to note that there are times that call for us to be passive. An example might be if we are being persecuted for our faith. Matthew 5:39b says, "...whosoever shall smite thee on the right cheek, turn to him the other also." There are other times when we need to decide if the issue is really worth addressing or if we can let it go.

There are also times when it seems necessary to be aggressive. Some people just do not get the message unless they hear it loud and clear, and perhaps with some force.

However, on the whole, assertiveness is the best behavior in all relationships. We don't think there is ever justification for being passive/aggressive.

BENEFITS OF LIVING ASSERTIVELY

Let's look at some of the ways that this positive outlook of assertiveness affects our thoughts, attitudes and relationships:

An assertive person is in control of their emotions; they will decide how to feel rather than allowing someone else to push their buttons, or nurture hurtful thoughts.

An assertive person does not avoid conflict; they know it is important to deal with issues so that they do not turn into bitterness or resentment. They will also be courageous enough to take the initiative to deal with these issues rather than wait for the other person to come to them. The assertive person knows that addressing issues is the best way to maintain healthy relationships.

In addressing those issues, the assertive person has learned to use questions rather than blaming or demanding. He can also brainstorm with others to focus on a solution, rather than dwelling on the problem; he is a good team player.

An assertive person learns to take action rather than nurturing hurtful thoughts and worrying endlessly. He has also learned to make better choices and to ask for God's help to overcome bad behaviors, including addictions.

An assertive person can be a good listener; he can hear the other person without becoming defensive or feeling that he has to justify his position. A person who is defensive about his behavior will seldom overcome addictions. An assertive person is willing to ask for help; having an accountability person can be very effective.

An assertive person takes responsibility for his actions and is willing to ask for forgiveness when they have wronged someone. They will also take steps not to repeat the behavior.

An assertive person is able to accept God's forgiveness, believing that he is fully forgiven; all guilt and shame is gone.

An assertive person can approach God boldly, knowing who he is in Christ and believing that God loves him and wants him to have an abundant life. He feels confident to ask for God's guidance and knows that he "...can do all things through Christ..." Philippians 4:13NKJV. God will give him the strength to do what he needs to do.

When assertiveness affects our thoughts, attitudes and emotions in a positive way, we know that it will also affect our health in positive ways. An assertive person often has a much healthier life, both emotionally and physically.

In our office we deal with a lot of people who are not assertive when they first come and our observations affirm that a lack of assertiveness leads to people being unwell. Medical science validates the fact that many of our physical and emotional illnesses have their root in our inner life. Often passive people don't feel worthy of standing up for themselves, and they end up feeling very discouraged and invalidated. Continually thinking negative thoughts can lead to depression.

In our counseling office, we assign the Taylor-Johnson Temperament Analysis test for all clients at the first session. When we graph the results, it is very common to see that clients who struggle with depression, also tend to be very passive and submissive. If we can help clients to learn how to be assertive, it will almost certainly result in a lessening of the client's depression.

Hanging onto hurtful thoughts and feelings can affect us in other ways as well. Clients with other serious illnesses have sometimes admitted that they have held a lot of resentment and bitterness inside, rather than addressing issues with others; this may well have contributed to the disease.

Again, it is so important for people to address hurtful issues so that they do not turn into bitterness and resentment. We will enjoy much better health, both emotionally and physically, when there are no reasons to hold grudges against anyone.

The angry thought life of an aggressive person may lead to various physical illnesses, according to medical research and because of their devious behavior, passive/aggressive people will deal with a lot of guilt, once again causing physical or emotional illness, unless the person deals with the guilt, and makes better choices. Again, the answer is assertiveness.

The Bible has a lot to say about how our feelings affect our health. Proverbs 15:13 says, "A merry heart makes a cheerful countenance, but by sorrow of the heart the spirit is broken." In Proverbs 17:22 we read, "A merry heart does good, like medicine, but a broken spirit dries the bones."

God knows the negative effect that anxiety can have on our spirits, so He says to us in Philippians 4:6 & 7, "Be anxious for nothing, but in everything by prayer and supplication, with thanksgiving, let your requests be made known to God; and the peace of God which surpasses all understanding, will guard your hearts and minds through Jesus Christ."

* * *

One of the families who came for counseling at our office can easily summarize the effects of a lack of assertiveness. The father had a very aggressive personality, his wife was very passive and their two teenage daughters were passive/aggressive. When challenged about his behavior in the counseling office, the father refused to take seriously the advice, even though it was based on Scripture. This was especially unusual since this man and his wife had made plans to go to another country as missionaries. He scoffed at the Bible verse he was asked to read, suggesting he needed to see it in the King James version. When that version was presented to him, he merely said, "So what!?"

As a passive person, his wife did not question his laws in their home, believing that she was being submissive. And the daughters were afraid of their father; they knew he would never let them go to parties held by their friends, so they snuck out their bedroom window.

There was very little progress in their counseling and soon they stopped coming. Quite some time later, the father called our office to let us know that his wife had died of cancer and they had not been able to go to the mission field. We encouraged him that it was not too late to change his ways and be there for his daughters.

This family's story could have ended differently if the father had admitted his aggressiveness and learned how to be assertive. If his wife had learned to come out of her passive state to assertively stand up for herself, she may have enjoyed good health for a long time, not to say that all sickness is a result of passivity but it does seem to make a difference. And if the daughters had seen true Christian, assertive behavior demonstrated by their parents, they could have made changes in their lives that would lead them into productive, happy lives.

Chapter III
THE "REST OF THE STORY"

Perhaps you'd like to know what happened to the people we introduced you to at the beginning of the book.

Louise realized that she could not go on this way. Somehow she got through the day, but she was determined that things would have to change.

She decided that if she indeed, would get nothing from the proceeds of their home, she would not let that stop her from doing something positive to create a better life for herself.

Louise had often considered getting some counseling, but she had never done so. Once she had even called an agency and booked an appointment. However, the day before her appointment, she called to cancel, using some phony excuse.

Now Louise decided that this would be her first goal; she would book an appointment, and this time she would keep it. That evening Louise carefully evaluated the different counseling offices that were listed in the yellow pages of the local telephone directory. After carefully reviewing their specialties and their locations, Louise settled on one that seemed like it would be the best fit.

Before she called to make an appointment, Louise hurried to the mall to pick up some toiletries that she needed for the next day. She had only taken a few things with her when she left her house and she was afraid to go back for the rest. At the mall she met an old friend, Sylvia, who suggested they chat over a cup of coffee.

Louise had always been a very private person, not wanting to share her private life with others. This evening, Louise couldn't hide the fact that she was not doing well. Having had very little sleep the night before, and worrying all day about her future, Louise looked at least ten years older than she really was, with worry lines casting deep shadows under her eyes.

When her friend asked how she was doing, Louise decided to come clean and tell her everything. She ended by telling Sylvia that she was considering some counseling. Her friend strongly encouraged this and told her about a counselor that had been recommended to her some time ago. She had not yet made an appointment for herself, but she encouraged Louise to call the office.

When Louise returned to her son's home, she looked up the counselor that Sylvia had recommended and found out that he worked out of the same office that she had settled on earlier.

First thing next morning, Louise called and booked an appointment. She had to wait two weeks to get in, but this time she kept the appointment. Minutes after the session started, Louise knew that the wait had definitely been worth it. She spilled out the whole story of her life and found a counselor who was willing to hear and empathize with her. She was pleasantly surprised to hear that her husband could not legally shut her out of receiving any of the proceeds of the sale of their home. But much more important was the fact that the counselor helped her to feel like she was not losing her mind and that she had some legitimate concerns about how she had been treated.

Louise met weekly with her counselor and learned that her past behavior was for the most part, passive behavior. She was very surprised to hear that the Bible actually encourages us to be assertive, to stand up for ourselves! Louise had always believed that it was the "Christian" thing to give in and to allow others to get their own way.

After several months of counseling, Louise called her husband, Tom, and let him know that she would not accept any more abusive behavior and that she wanted her share of the proceeds from the sale of their home. Most of all, she told him that she still loved him and wanted things to work out between them.

It took many months, but eventually Tom joined Louise in the counseling sessions where Tom learned that his behavior was aggressive. They learned that both passive and aggressive behavior is not helpful in relationships and neither behavior is pleasing to God.

The counselor helped them dig out the roots of their dysfunctional behavior, and helped them to realize that they truly loved each other. Both Tom and Louise needed to learn better ways of communicating with each other, and showing respect to one another.

Six months later, Louise moved back home and she and Tom are continuing to work on improving their marriage relationship. Both Tom and Louise look forward to the best years of their entire marriage!

Jack spent most of the evening in his study. His wife came to ask him to come to the dining room for dinner, but Jack refused, saying he wasn't hungry. Jack decided that if his co-workers thought he was abusive and impatient, he would be even more so in the days ahead.

Jack went to work early the next day and when the rest of the employees in his department arrived, he called for a departmental meeting. In the meeting, Jack announced new assignments and due dates that were even more unrealistic than in the past.

Jack's co-workers were disappointed that Jack was responding in this way, but there wasn't much they could do about it; he was their supervisor after all. Jack became increasingly demanding and critical when supervising their work.

Eventually, everyone in the department except Jack met at a local diner, to discuss their situation. They decided to talk to the boss and let him know that unless Jack left the company, they would all resign, effectively immediately.

Jack's boss was very disappointed to hear that Jack had not learned from the evaluation and that instead, he accelerated his abusive behavior. He knew that Jack was very gifted as an accountant and he hated to lose him, but he also knew it was not fair to keep him on. The following Friday, Jack's boss called him in and gave him the news that he was letting him go. Jack pleaded to keep his job, but his boss would not change his mind.

Jack stopped in at the bar near his house, before going home to tell his wife what had happened. As he sat at the bar, sipping his beer, the light went on. He had thought that he could force others to comply with his demands. He realized now that he had not considered how things felt from his co-workers point of view.

Jack applied for a job at many different offices, but it seemed that his reputation went ahead of him. Finally, Jack had been out of work for six months and their savings were dwindling.

Jack had always considered counseling to be something that only weak people would do. He felt that he was the master of his own fate, and he didn't need anyone to tell him how to live his life. Now however, Jack began to wonder if there might be some benefit in talking to someone. He called the office where one of his friends had gone while going through a divorce, and booked an appointment with a counselor.

Jack met weekly with his counselor and learned that since he had grown up with a very domineering father who never let him express his opinion, he had become domineering himself, now that he was an adult. As a child, he had felt weak, with no right to speak or do things, unless his father gave him permission. He had hated being so weak, but now as an adult, he picked on other weak people because he knew they would not resist him.

Eventually Jack learned that he could be assertive instead of aggressive, and this would not be a position of weakness, but neither would it be a position of domination. As an assertive person, he could respect others, while at the same time, ask for respect for himself.

Jack was so excited to learn how effective assertive communication and behavior was, he learned quickly to change his ways.

A month later, Jack received a call back from one of the offices where he had sent his resume, asking to interview him for a position with the company. Excitedly, Jack went to the interview, and with his self-confidence restored, had a good interview. He treated the person interviewing him with respect and he also did not hesitate to promote himself, knowing he was very good at his job. Jack was hired and is currently enjoying his new position, determined to treat his co-workers with the respect and dignity that they deserve.

But work is not the only place where Jack is having better relationships; life at home with his wife and son has greatly improved. No longer does his wife cringe when she hears his car in the driveway and his son runs to greet him when he walks in the door. Jack makes sure he hugs his son and spends some time playing with him before the family sits down to dinner. After dinner, Jack likes to sit and talk to his wife, finding out about her day.

Old habits die hard, and Jack goes back to talk to his counselor every now and then, just to keep a check on his attitudes and actions. Overall, Jack is a much happier man now that he has learned that assertiveness gets him the respect that he always wanted as an aggressive man!

Samantha went to the concert. Everyone around her seemed to be having a great time, but Samantha felt strangely empty of all emotion. If she felt anything at all, it was remorse. Her mother had always been there for her, and she realized she had not treated her right.

Samantha mulled these thoughts over and over in her mind, but realized there was nothing she could do about it right now. All at once, her friend Julie, elbowed her in the ribs and shouted over the music, "Hey Sam! What's wrong with you?! Here we are at a great concert, and you look like you've lost your last friend!"

Samantha smiled weakly at her friend and tried to get in the mood of the concert, but it was no use. She decided she would try to get through this evening, later she would apologize to her mother, and try to make it up to her.

On the ride home, Todd pulled out a can of beer from under the seat, pulled the tab, and started drinking. Samantha couldn't believe he would drink and drive; she should have listened to her mother. She glanced at Julie, in the front seat beside Todd, to see how she was feeling about this. She didn't seem the least bit concerned and continued to sing along with the concert group's latest CD which Todd had purchased and was playing on the car stereo.

Samantha tapped Todd on the shoulder and tried to talk to him about drinking and driving. Todd shrugged his shoulder and said, "If you don't like my driving, I'd be happy to stop the car and let you out." Samantha knew she couldn't possibly do that; they were still twenty miles from home, so she leaned back in the seat and tried to get comfortable.

Her seat belt was digging into her side, so she loosened it and pulled out more length. Just as she did this, Todd swerved to miss a big deer starting to cross the highway. He slammed his foot on the brakes but it was too late to miss the deer, which landed on the hood of the car, denting it, and breaking the windshield.

Glass from the windshield landed on everyone in the car, including Samantha. She had not had time to fasten her seatbelt, and as a result, she was thrown across the back seat and hit her head hard, on the opposite window. She was knocked unconscious and when she came to, she was in an ambulance, with the sirens screaming. Samantha was hurting everywhere, but her worst pain was in knowing how upset her mother would be.

Samantha spent several weeks in the hospital during which time she and her mother had lots of opportunities to talk. She told her mother everything and promised to do things differently in the future.

Samantha's mother also arranged some counseling for both of them, where they learned a lot about themselves. Samantha's mother realized that her guilt had led her to be more lenient with Samantha than was healthy, and Samantha learned that by doing things behind her mother's back, and lying to her, she was being passive/aggressive. Samantha also realized that her mother was very wise, and that she needed to be open with her and listen to her advice.

Samantha and her mother continued their counseling sessions, sometimes individually, and sometimes jointly. They learned much about their styles of behavior, and learned that when they both talked and acted assertively, their relationship was one of harmony and peace for the most part.

Samantha is still a teenager so she reverts at times to immature behavior, but at these times, her mother realizes it is her responsibility to be the mature person, and to give Samantha firm guidelines. She has also learned to give Samantha appropriate consequences when her teenage hormones have led her astray.

Samantha has also learned to be assertive with her friends, saying "No" to doing things that she knows would get her in trouble.

Chapter IV
ASSERTIVENESS ACROSTIC

We have talked about numerous aspects of assertiveness. All are important and we hope you will read and reread the whole book to get a deeper understanding of assertiveness. However, we also want to give you a quick reference so that you can quickly recall how to handle situations as they arise by memorizing one or two main words for each letter in the word, "Assertiveness".

A – ASK QUESTIONS – JESUS DID!

ADDRESS ISSUES

S – STAND UP FOR YOUR NEEDS AND CONVICTIONS

S – SPECIFY WHAT YOU WILL AND WILL NOT PUT UP WITH - I.E. SET BOUNDARIES

E – EVALUATE THE IMPORTANCE OF HOW AND WHAT YOU WILL ADDRESS

EXPRESS YOUR FEELINGS IN ACCEPTABLE WAYS

R – RESPECT OTHERS AND ASK FOR RESPECT

T – THINK BEFORE YOU ACT AND SPEAK

TAKE RESPONSIBILITY FOR YOUR WORDS AND ACTIONS

I – INITIATE ACTION INSTEAD OF REACTING LATER

USE "I" SENTENCES

V – VERIFY WHAT YOU ARE BEING ACCUSED OF

VALUE RELATIONSHIPS AND CHOOSE TO FORGIVE OTHERS

E – ENCOURAGE OTHERS

N – NEGOTIATE TO RESOLVE ISSUES

E – EXAMPLE OF JESUS IN SCRIPTURE

S – SELF-WORTH AS A RESULT OF BEING ASSERTIVE

S – SERVICE TO OTHERS FOLLOWS ASSERTIVENESS

Bibliography

Burns, David D., M.D., <u>The Feeling Good Handbook</u>, William Morrow and Company, Inc., 105 Madison Ave.. New York, N.Y. 10016 © 1989 by David D. Burns, M.D.

Viktor E. Frankl , <u>Man's Search for Meaning,</u> Washington Square Press, Inc., 630 Fifth Avenue, New York, N.Y. Copyright (c) 1959, 1963, by Viktor E. Frankl, All rights reserved, Printed in the U.S.A.

Barbara Colorosa, <u>kids are worth it! GIVING YOUR CHILD THE GIFT OF INNER DISCIPLINE</u>, Published in Penguin Books, 1999, Published in this edition, 2001, Copyright © Barbara Colorosa, 1994, 2001

John Burke, <u>Soul Revolution,</u> Zondervan Grand Rapids, Michigan 49530, Copyright © 2008 by John Burke

Donna Carter, <u>10 Smart Things Women Can Do to Build a Better Life,</u> Published in 2006 by Straight Talk Books, 38 River Rock Cres. S.E. Calgary, Alberta T2C 4J4 Copyright © by Donna Carter

Melody Beattie, <u>Codependent No More, How to Stop Controlling Others and Start Caring For Yourself</u>, Hazelden

Poems